HOW TO GET YOUR SELF-PUBLISHED BOOK INTO BOOKSTORES

DEBBIE YOUNG

Series Editor
ORNA ROSS

How to Get Your Self-Published Book into Bookstores

An Alliance of Independent Authors Guide: Successful Self-Publishing Series Book 4

Copyright © 2017 Debbie Young, Orna Ross, The Alliance of Independent Authors

ISBN ebook: 978-1-909888-48-7

ISBN POD Edition: 978-1-909888-49-4

Published by Font Publications, London, UK 2017

This version with minor revisions and updated glossary November 2017

Category: Writing, Publishing

Cover Art: © Dmitri Malinovski

Cover Design: Andrew Brown at Design for Writers

Editorial: Brett Hardman, Margaret Hunter

Formatting and Interior Design: Margaret Hunter at Daisy Editorial

10 9 8 7 6 5 4 3 2 1

CONTENTS

DEFINITIONS AND TERMS OF REFERENCE

"You say bookstore, I say bookshop…" Before we get started, let's set some definitions to avoid confusion further down the line.

I happen to be British, but I'm also a member of the Alliance of Independent Authors (ALLi), a truly global online organization whose members learn from each other's experience and share best self-publishing practice around the world. Throughout this book (and with apologies in advance to any UK, African, or Australian booksellers who would never refer to their place of work this way), I therefore use the more common international term "bookstore" rather than British "bookshop" to refer to a physical shop.

In publishing and the book trade "bricks-and-mortar shops" or "brick-stores" are terms often used to mean a physical place, as opposed to an online retailer. Such stores almost always have an online presence too, with websites used to order books for home delivery or, currently a growing trend, to fuel a click-and-collect service. These days, a bookstore without a website is not likely to last long.

For ease of reference, in this book physical stores are called **bookstores** in contrast to retailers who sell solely online, which are referred to as **online book retailers**.

The largest of such, of course, is Amazon, which is currently testing a new business model of bookstore. Built around the power of Amazon's reader, Kindle, each store stocks 6,000 online bestsellers.

The number of Amazon's physical bookstores is expected to grow, but for the foreseeable future we can expect its main revenue to be online. Therefore, in these pages, we consider Amazon to be an online retailer for now.

What Is an Independent Bookstore?

Bookstores fall within two broad categories: bookstore chains, in which a board of directors or other central body manages a group of stores, usually from a head office, to an often unified sales and business structure; and independents, or indie bookstores, which are one-off shops or very small chains.

Again, borderlines are blurry. There are chains that like to consider themselves indie, because they are mold-breaking, innovative, and maverick. James Daunt, MD of a large British chain of bookstores, Waterstones, has described himself as "an independent bookseller who just happens to be running a chain" (*The Bookseller*, 13 November 2015).

Hmm…

While it's possible to be both a chain and independent of thought, when we talk about independent bookstores in this book, we mean the one-off shops. There are, though, a few indie bookstores with more than one branch. In the ever more creative business of bookselling, nothing is straightforward.

What we do *not* mean, though, by independent bookstores is those stores that stock only self-published books. These are a separate category of independent store, which is described in detail in the chapter "Different Types of Bookstore."

Other Kinds of Stores That Sell Books

To further complicate matters, not all stores that sell books, on or offline, are bookstores. Depending on the kind of book you write, you may be keen to target specialist retailers whose customer profiles match that of your target reader.

Nonspecialist retailers selling books, sometimes called "special sales" in the trade, is another growing trend.

A small, carefully curated stock of books can perfectly supplement the ethos of a fashion or lifestyle brand. As in the old adage that "books furnish a room," the right mix of books can be used as a shorthand to demonstrate a shop's philosophy and character to the casual observer, such as Cordon Bleu recipe books in an upmarket kitchen shop, or style guides in a fashion retailer. These are considered as opportunities for indie authors separately in the chapter "Different Types of Bookstore".

Booksellers Versus Bookstore Staff

I'll refer to the specialist staff who work in bookstores, i.e. the personnel who advise customers and take their money, as booksellers, rather than any of the other terms that are often used—sales advisers, shop assistants, counter staff, etc.

It's important to recognize that, in good bookstores, the staff are far more than just counter assistants ringing up sales, or *beepeuses* as the French so beautifully put it, the term named after the beeping sound of the supermarket checkout barcode scanner.

A bookseller is a specialist who:

- cares about the market sector
- loves books and reading
- is hugely knowledgeable about reading trends and habits
- is passionate about uniting customers with books that will excite them.

An indie author seeking to place books in a bookstore must never underestimate the skills and importance of individual booksellers. Having such a person behind your book can make an enormous difference.

All proprietors are likely to be booksellers, but not all booksellers are proprietors. Where I mean specifically a bookseller who owns an indie bookstore, I'll call them the proprietor. When I use the word "bookseller," on the other hand, I'll mean any customer-facing member of staff who works in the bookstore, which may or may not be the proprietor in an indie bookstore.

For the sake of simplicity, I'll also, incidentally, use "they" and "them" when talking about authors, booksellers, readers, and other generic groups in the singular. It makes for much easier reading than using "he or she."

WHY THIS BOOK IS NEEDED

Once upon a time, bookstores were just about the only place that books were sold, in a choice of two formats: paperback or hardback. Then along came four revolutions:

- **Online shopping:** The arrival of the internet made online shopping from home not only possible but also popular, with books a particularly suitable commodity for this route, being easy to pack and mail, unbreakable in transit, and of consistent quality wherever you buy them.
- **Print-on-demand (POD) services:** Advances in digital printing technology made it possible for the first time to print good-quality books at a viable unit cost for resale at a profit in very short print runs.
- **Online publishing services:** The launch of various services enabled aspiring self-publishing authors to write, edit, design, format, and upload books without leaving their desk. However, ALLi recommends outsourcing any tasks in which you can't achieve a professional standard yourself to provide a top-quality end product.
- **The ereader:** First emerging in the form of a dedicated

ereader, quickly joined by ereading apps for your preferred digital device, the ereader created a whole new market, offering indie authors a new low-cost, high-profit route to get their work in front of readers around the world at the touch of a button.

These developments have shaken up the old world of bookselling on a seismic scale, introducing a whole new world of competition that bypasses traditional publishing houses.

Booksellers are not Luddites—don't forget their business is powered by sophisticated just-in-time stock control and ordering systems—but many were concerned that the brave new ebook world would erode their core business.

Many self-publishing authors, particularly early adopters of the new technology, decided to bypass print books altogether, given the higher potential profit margins on ebooks, whose production costs were entirely front-loaded, and whose delivery and inventory costs were nil.

Those indie authors who did embrace print, via POD services, often found it nigh on impossible to get their books into bookstores, which were entirely geared up to dealing only with big publishing houses.

A few bookstores gamely tried to make inroads into selling ebooks and ereaders, but with little success. Some commentators identified a further new development, the Espresso Book Machine, as a means by which booksellers could embrace the digital arena. These sophisticated digital printers are able to produce POD books on the spot, drawing content from remote databases, in the time that it takes to brew a cup of coffee.

Enthusiasts (and sales staff) suggested the technology would also empower booksellers to produce books whose content was in the public domain, such as out-of-copyright classics, at a substantial markup. A further market would be high-value, low-volume publications such as academic theses.

In theory, this sounded promising. The Espresso would allow the bookstore to become a direct producer and distributor, while offering the reader instant access to digitally printed books within their local physical bookstore, cutting out the internet intermediary.

Unfortunately, the enormous cost of these highly sophisticated machines is way beyond the budget of the average bookstore. Return on investment is long and slow, even in highly populous cities, never mind issues of maintenance and repair, compared with the relatively simple photocopier. No surprises, then, that this has not proved to be a fairy godmother for bookstores, enabling them to leap aboard the digital revolution.

While there are more than five Espresso Book Machines in action, at the time of writing, the number of installations hovers just north of three figures worldwide. I am reminded, however, of the notorious statement by early IBM president Thomas Watson in 1947: "I think there is a world market for maybe five computers."

Although the initial hysteria has died down, not least because experience has taught us that ebooks don't spell the death of print, nor online stores the end of physical bookstores, there is still a lack of understanding and common ground between bookstores and self-published authors.

Sadly, this has prompted some authors to give up on bookstores altogether, and some bookstores are known to have implemented a blanket ban on indie authors' books.

At ALLi, we have seen that, where booksellers and authors understand each other's needs and practices, there is a third way for indie authors and bookstores to work together for mutual benefit. This goes much further than simply stocking self-published books on their shelves.

This book is designed to help indie authors step back from the emotional debates and dramatic, headline-grabbing claims made by the press or inferred from the information (and often misinformation) on the internet. It provides context and background to facilitate open discussion and respectful, informed relationships between author and bookseller.

While many authors want to see their book in bookstores without fully understanding why—for example, because of a love of the stores, because of an assumption that's how books are sold—we encourage authors to step back and understand their motives.

Don't let bookstore aspirations blind you to the opportunities you have to find your readers through other, equally good, if not more successful, distribution channels. Rather than "How can I get my book into a bookstore?," the first question you should ask is "How can I use my position as a self-publisher as an advantage to sell copies of my book?" For most indies, bookstore distribution is something to think about after you have already successfully sold books online, not before.

When that time comes, the information and advice in these pages will help independent authors to approach bookstores confidently and competently, and to foster long-term relationships that will help both parties thrive in a spirit of cooperation and collaboration. And, though aimed at authors, it will help any bookseller who reads it to understand that good self-published books are an opportunity that can represent more income per title and a more direct connection with authors.

Such creative and commercial opportunities are, of course, in the best interest of that most important person for all concerned: the reader.

ABOUT THE #AUTHORS4BOOKSTORES CAMPAIGN

I n 2015, in the appropriate setting of a historic London bookstore's flagship premises (Foyles, Charing Cross Road), ALLi announced its **#Authors4Bookstores** campaign. The purpose of this campaign is to encourage interested authors and bookstores to work together for mutual benefit.

The #Authors4Bookstores campaign was first mooted by historical novelist Piers Alexander, an indie author who has built a strong relationship with bookstores, in particular winning a deal to place his debut novel, *The Bitter Trade*, in the high-traffic travel stores of major British bookstore chain, WHSmith.

Space in such compact stores is so limited that it will always be reserved for the lucky few, who are almost always authors published by one of the "Big Five" publishing companies. Piers's experience shows that, with focus, determination, and the facts at your fingertips, it is possible to get self-published books into bookstores on an equal footing with trade-published books.

Yet most indie authors do not even consider trying to sell their books through bookstores:

- they prefer to focus on ebooks for a simpler life

- they publish print copies but have been unable to find a profitable means of selling them via bookstores
- they prefer the larger margin and lower production cost of ebooks
- they've tried it, but made a loss, due to the high margins expected by booksellers and the impact of sale or return losses
- they've been unable to persuade any bookstores to stock their books
- they haven't dared approach bookstores, for fear of a rebuff
- they assume bookstores don't stock self-published books on principle so don't bother asking.

We believe that indie authors whose books are published to professional standards (which ALLi encourages them to aim for) should feel comfortable and confident about presenting their books for consideration for sale in bookstores, should they wish to do so. One key purpose of this book is therefore to help indie authors navigate the right course to place their books in stores.

The Author's Prerogative

There may be, however, many good reasons why an author prefers to sell solely through other means, such as online retail stores or hand-selling at events. At ALLi, we firmly believe that it is the author's prerogative to choose their own retail route, and there are no absolute rights and wrongs. Authors who sell well online, whether ebook only or also in print, may prefer to keep their working practices simple, and their profits optimal, by not venturing into physical bookstores. Less admin means more time to write more books.

What we want to do is ensure that every author has given bookstores due consideration, and to give those authors who do decide to partner with bookstores the confidence that they've made that decision for the right reasons, and not out of fear, misunderstanding, or lack of knowledge.

Synergy with Bookstores

We also believe that there is a natural synergy between indie authors and indie bookstores, not only due to their obvious shared love of connecting readers with books, but in many other ways, as discussed in the chapter "Other Ways of Selling Books In-Store". If you don't want to take advantage of this synergy, that's up to you—but we don't want you to miss out on a growing range of exciting opportunities in bookstores for lack of information or inspiration.

Not Only for Indies

As a global organization representing indie authors, ALLi naturally focuses on the self-publishing sector. However, much of the content and principles in this book, and within the #Authors4Bookstores campaign as a whole, is equally applicable to trade-published authors, many of whom are also less engaged than they might be with bookstores. Of course, there is less financial incentive for a trade-published author, as the royalty is significantly lower, but we believe that authors of all kinds, no matter how they are published, benefit from working closely with bookstores.

A Practical Campaign

The #Authors4Bookstores campaign therefore aims to build collaboration between authors of all kinds and bookstores by creating better mutual understanding and awareness, and by dispelling any nervousness about engaging with each other. As a part of that campaign, this book provides not just a call to action, but also practical advice for authors such as:

- helpful insights into how bookstores operate
- advice on how to make your book bookstore ready
- guidelines on how to approach bookstores

- practical tips about the most effective supply chain for your needs
- inspiring case studies from authors working successfully with bookstores.

The Right Time

Why now? Over the past few years, there has been much reporting about the collective health of bookstores, but if as indie authors we work together with booksellers, we can only improve prospects for all of us. It's a complex picture, with very different scenarios around the world.

In some countries, the number of bookstores is on a healthy upward trend, whether or not bolstered by national pricing legislation that eliminates the undercutting of prices by bigger retailers that elsewhere threatens smaller traders. In others, there have been dramatic declines, whether steadily or sporadically.

Around the world, some commentators, in particular general media that always love a scaremongering story, have suggested that the decline of bookstores is inevitable, thanks to two parallel modern revolutions: the rise of online retailers and the emergence of ebooks. It's been relatively easy for reporters to field heartrending case studies of booksellers of forty years' standing having to close their store for lack of a buyer.

The press are also quick to embrace surveys undertaken by parties with a vested interest likely to skew the results, provided they make good headlines, and not only in stories regarding the book trade. These include surveys that indicate the plateauing or reduction of ebook sales, compared with print books. Drilling down into their source data reveals that they are leaving self-published ebooks out of the equation, as ALLi founder and director Orna Ross explained in an opinion piece on the Self-Publishing Advice Blog.

There have also been plenty of predictions that books are an endangered species, public appetite being diverted by the many other sources of entertainment and relaxation.

But the real situation is more encouraging. While some bookstores close, new bookstores are springing up, or old ones are being reinvigorated by exciting initiatives that fit them well to the needs of the twenty-first-century reader.

The more successful chains are expanding, new players are entering the field, often from outside of the traditional bookstore arena, and the notion of a modern bookstore is fast evolving to become a more exciting, dynamic, and thriving arena.

Retail was ever thus. Business was ever thus. While it's true that many bookstores have closed, with plenty of neighborhoods losing their sole remaining bookstore, that's true across many retail sectors —fashion, sports, household goods, etc.—as retailing trends continue to evolve. It would be astonishing if it were not so with booksellers trading unchanged from decade to decade.

Traders large and small come and go. Those who are able to read the signs of change in an ever-evolving marketplace stay ahead of the game. Those who are less farsighted or more conservative fall by the wayside.

Authors who recognize and embrace the change in bookstores will have the opportunity to form relationships with the successful traders, and to jump aboard their ship to sail into a brighter future.

If bookstores are evolving from old-style purveyors of books to multifaceted cultural centers celebrating reading and writing, it's great news for authors, especially those who embrace change opportunistically and who think outside the box. We'll be sharing a taster of such developments in the chapter "Bookstores, Past, Present, and Future"—and if you're not already convinced that you want to be part of the bookstore scene, we hope you will be by the end of that section. But if not—well, that's your choice, and we support that too!

A Broader Principle

Whatever lies ahead for bookstores, we believe that their continuing existence benefits all authors. If all authors support bookstores in as many ways as they are able, the stores' future will be brighter. As we'll see in the chapter "How I Do It", there are dozens of ways you can support bookstores, even if you choose not to sell your books via that route, and most of these ways won't cost you a penny.

The #Authors4Bookstores campaign therefore isn't only about gaining retail shelf space for self-published books and helping bookstores build profit for all parties. It also addresses the broader issue of the value to authors of visible, physical bookstores within our society and our communities. We believe the presence of bookstores in our shopping malls and on our main streets and our high streets, all around the world, helps create a richer cultural environment and fosters a love of books in society as a whole. We have therefore included:

- tips on other ways to work effectively with booksellers besides getting your books on their shelves
- easy ways to support bookstores at little or no cost.

Wherever you stand on the issues outlined above, we hope you will at least invest the small amount of time required to read this book. Then, if you still choose to give bookstores a wide berth, that's your right as an indie, and that right is something that ALLi would defend to the death.

So, in short, this guidebook, *How to Get Your Self-Published Book into Bookstores,* is being produced as an instrument of the #Authors4Bookstores campaign to help authors and bookstores work together for mutual benefit. It provides a reality check on the feasibility of selling self-published books in bookstores, inside information to give you a better understanding of how bookstores operate, and practical advice to help you do what it says on the cover —to sell your self-published books in bookstores—should you decide that's what you'd like to do.

But before we go any further, let's kick off with an examination of what constitutes a bookstore, both historically and in the present, and what it might become in the future.

BOOKSTORES, PAST, PRESENT, AND FUTURE

 ew indie authors would disagree with the popular maxims "Self-publishing isn't a sprint, it's a marathon" or "We're in it for the long-haul." But given our self-governing status, we expect to be able to make things happen relatively quickly, from uploading our carefully formatted files for publication online to adding a new cover or revising the blurb for our books, to temporarily reducing the retail price of a book to create a special offer. We are, after all, independent: we are our own publishers.

However, when it comes to bookstores, we do not call the shots. Rather, we are dependent on the way the bookstores work. If we want our books to fit in and flourish, we must comply with the constraints. Each author is only a tiny cog in the vast machinery. To stand the best chance of success in getting our books stocked in bookstores, we need to step back for a moment and consider how they operate, to view the bookstore from the bookseller's side of the counter.

In addition to reading this book, you might also:

- read booksellers' memoirs
- read novels set in bookstores and/or written by authors

with bookselling experience (you'll find a recommended
further reading list in the Appendix of this book)
- work in a bookstore as an intern, temp or part-time
assistant
- befriend and chat to your local bookseller, asking questions
about the business (just be careful to pick a time when the
store is quiet so as not to affect trade)
- watch comedy classics such as the TV series *Black Books* or
the bookstore sketch in Marty Feldman's "Marty Amok"
show (easy to find on YouTube)
- watch movies set in bookstores such as *Notting Hill* and
You've Got Mail (for more ideas, see
bookriot.com/2013/a/30/16-movies-starring-bookstores).

The Bookstore Past

You can find a long and fascinating history of the book trade in its
various forms in Lewis Buzbee's *The Yellow-Lighted Bookshop*, but, for a
bit of fun, let's start with an extract from an ALLi author's historical
novel set in an eighteenth-century London bookstore. The joy of
print-on-demand, which twenty-first-century authors take for
granted, is put into perspective by this affectionate passage in
Lucienne Boyce's novel *To The Fair Land* describing a chaotic scene
from an era in which books were still handprinted by letterpress. To
secure his copy of a bestseller by a mysterious anonymous author, the
hero, Ben Dearlove, along with other would-be purchasers, has to
wait while it is printed. The opening scene of chapter 4 is reminiscent
of a modern Black Friday superstore scuffle:

*Who would have thought that book lovers could be so warlike? They
jammed themselves around Mr Dowling's door, ignoring the fact that
six people could not pass through a space wide enough for two, dealing
out spiteful jabs and sly blows to one another. The stationer,
watchmaker and music seller stood on their own doorsteps, complaining*

loudly about the crowd that made it impossible for their customers to pass.

Ben Dearlove comes to the rescue of the besieged bookseller, Mr Dowling. On reaching the front of the queue, he ducked down and crawled under the girl's skirts, at which she set up a greater shrieking than ever. Emerging on the other side of her lumpy knees, he slithered under the table, struggled to his feet, snatched An Account of a Voyage to the Fair Land from His Lordship's footman and clambered onto the table.

"Ladies and Gentlemen!" he bellowed. "If you have a ticket, please wait on this side of the shop. If you have not yet put your name down for a copy, please move to the right and Sam will come round and make a note of your details. Tickets only on this side... Yes, sir, every printing machine between here and London Wall is rattling off copies as we speak... No, madam, to the right if you wish to put your name down."

"Mr Dearlove!" Dowling gazed up at the young man in grateful surprise. "Thank heaven! I did not think I could withstand the siege much longer!"

— Lucienne Boyce, To The Fair Land

While delivery from publisher to reader became less fraught in time, particularly with the coming of the railways, the supply chain remained, until recently, dictated by publishers and their printing schedules. This included the control of selling prices. Minimum prices of books were determined by publishing houses, and in many countries book prices were protected against discounting by law. (In many countries they still are, preventing the erosion of publishers' profits and therefore, in theory at least, author earnings.) Each new book had to be printed in large quantities, typically high hundreds and even thousands, to arrive at a marketable unit cost. Part of the publisher's responsibility was to warehouse inventory to be called off as required by individual bookstores.

Until the 1930s, books were sold almost exclusively in bookstores, in hardback, on the publishers' terms, at relatively high prices. Buying books was considered a luxury, and lending libraries the only means for many people to obtain books to enjoy at home.

Then came the paperback revolution in the 1930s, fueled by Allen Lane, founder of Penguin Books, who was seeking a way of putting high-quality but affordable paperbacks into the hands of the masses for the equivalent price of a packet of cigarettes.

In the fortunate position of having prices protected from competition, booksellers could stock books safe in the knowledge that no one could buy them elsewhere at a lower cost. There were also some subscription services by post, offering club editions of books, but these were of limited lists of club editions not available in stores.

Toward the end of the twentieth century, in some countries, such a restrictive practice had started to be regarded as more of an unfair cartel, mitigating against the end user, the reader, in order to protect all other parties in the deal. It was therefore removed.

Such liberation freed bookstores to compete on price with each other, an action which particularly benefited the new bookstore chains that rose up in the late twentieth century. However, it also caused the sector to be targeted by much larger players in retailing, such as vast grocery superstore chains, luring book buyers away from traditional stores, at least for the cherry-picked bestsellers list that they deigned to stock.

More threatening still, in the case of online book retailers, with unlimited virtual shelf space, bookstores faced competition across their range, at least in terms of stock, if not customer service. While price protection was in place, the bookseller's main concern was to curate appropriate stock for local clientele, run the store efficiently, and treat customers well enough to make them want to patronize that store rather than anyone else's.

After all, customers had no alternative, other than to defect to a different bookstore or to borrow the book from their public library. If you wanted to buy a book, you went to a bookstore. If the bookseller was obliging and knowledgeable, well and good. If not, in the pre-internet age, when you couldn't "Google a book" or look it up in seconds on Amazon, finding a chosen title could be a challenge.

The circumstances that book buyers would put up with in order to buy their books were remarkable by today's standards. An example is Foyles' legendary Charing Cross Road store, then set in a rabbit warren of a building (across two buildings, in fact), where books were generally ordered by publisher rather than genre. When you did find one you wanted to buy, you had to visit two separate service counters in different places in the store to secure your purchase. Even so, customers adored the shop and were hugely loyal.

My mother used to work there in the 1950s, and when I described to her the wonderful new flagship store, designed in consultation with customers to make a highly enjoyable shopping experience, she said, "That's a shame. I rather liked the old way!" She tells a captivating story of how even staff discounts were arrived at erratically. Each Friday, staff presented their choice of books to the store's director, the elderly Miss Christina Foyle, who decided on an individual basis what discount each person should receive.

Interestingly, some of the most innovative new stores are now making a point of difference of sorting and displaying their books in unconventional categories, to add an element of excitement and surprise for browsers.

In those days, bookselling was perceived almost as a profession, and the bookseller respected as a knowledgeable and well-read cultural adviser.

In his introduction to Penelope Fitzgerald's poignant novel *The Bookstore*, set in the 1950s, novelist David Nicholls recalls:

For several years in the mid-1990s, I worked in a West London bookstore... My colleagues for the most part were English Literature graduates or postgraduates, knowledgeable and passionate about the written word. Yes, we were shop assistants but the fact that we sold books, as opposed to socks or potatoes or saucepans, gave the job a certain respectability, kudos almost... Books mattered, they were different, they were improving.

— DAVID NICHOLLS

The Bookstore Present

Fast forward to the twenty-first century, and the trading context for the average bookstore is very different.

In many countries, publishers are no longer able to fix prices, and may even be forbidden by law to do so. Publishers negotiate with chain stores to produce special editions of cherry-picked bestsellers to retail at bargain prices in grocery superstores. While the downward spiral in prices may benefit readers, boost numbers sold of the titles affected, and arguably draw in new readers, this situation creates new challenges for traditional booksellers struggling to compete with discounted top-selling titles. Bookstores enjoy greater stability in countries that still have fixed pricing for books.

The size, structure, and setup of stores has changed radically during living memory, with the rise of out-of-town shopping malls housing much bigger stores than are found in traditional city-center shopping areas. The buying experience in larger stores brings different challenges for the bookseller—more staff, a larger clientele, but less of a community feel or opportunity to recognize and bond with individual staff members.

In the small indie booksellers near me, I'm greeted by name the minute I enter the door, and I have long and interesting conversations with the single staff member who is usually on duty. In one of the bigger city-center stores, I wouldn't recognize the staff, there are so many on their rota, and would never expect them to recognize me. Having a conversation while they are ringing up my purchase on their till is unlikely: they are too busy.

While most big chains will try to engage with customers by offering some kind of loyalty scheme, the modern, more cynical customer is aware that such schemes exist not so much to serve the customer as to inform the company of the individual's buying habits and so target them with the most likely offers to convert into actual sales, just as online retailers do. It's not the same.

Large chains perceived as mainstays of the high street and shopping mall may have had to cut costs to keep their businesses viable. Staff budgets have been particularly vulnerable, and in some stores this has meant pegging staff pay, and reducing shop floor staff numbers and training costs. The variation in staff quality struck home with me when I asked a member of staff in a large bookstore that also sold newsstand publications whether it stocked *The Bookseller*, the UK book trade's publication. The staff member had never heard of it. That spoke volumes to me about the investment being placed in shop floor staff in this particular bookstore chain.

There are, of course, lots of good things about these bigger stores that enhance the customer experience (though some may make the author's heart sink): more space for a much greater product range, including diversification into nonbook products (usually those with higher profit margins such as stationery and gifts); coffee shops; browsing areas with comfy sofas; event areas; and, in countries where there is no fixed pricing, special offers that are negotiated with publishers, such as 3-for-2 offers and large discounting. Publishers also often buy guaranteed display space in high-traffic areas such as tabletops or outward-facing prime spot shelves.

The impact of online book retailers like Amazon, Flipcart, and The Book Depository on the fortunes of traditional bookstores is obvious. Big-box book retailers like Barnes & Noble in the US, Chapters in Canada, and Dymocks in Australia may have once driven small, independent booksellers out of business, but today in the shadow of ebooks and online retail, even megachains are suffering.

Online retailers have provided a convenient alternative for a public that spends an ever-increasing amount of time online in the comfort of their own home or workplace. They make it easier to browse stock at any time of day or night, because these stores are not hampered by opening and closing times, or the need to shut the doors at night to vacuum the carpets and replenish the bookshelves. They make it relatively easy to find the book you're looking for, or to suggest titles on the subject that you are seeking if you don't have a specific book in mind, (though less sensitively than if done by human advisers), using carefully calculated algorithms, bolstered by analytical data of what is currently selling well.

They also make impulse purchases more tempting by flagging up to readers what else they might like based on their current or previous orders. Bookstores cannot compete with that: their counters by the till may be stocked with high-margin impulse extra buys such as bookmarks and stationery, but these don't change to match each customer's historic buying pattern.

Not only do online retailers tempt the browser with clever arrays of appropriate products, they also, most importantly, cut prices. Special offers may even be set up without the publisher or self-published author knowing in advance. The price cuts on new launches of likely bestsellers, such as much-heralded celebrity autobiographies or the next big blockbuster from a top fiction author, will often be reduced beyond what conventional bookstores might offer. Amazon can afford to do this simply because it is confident that it will sell such vast numbers. (It's the same economy of scale that enables those companies that bring round little catalogs to places of work, listing a very small number of new and top-selling books at much reduced prices.)

Amazon's pricing policy has created an expectation among the book-buying public and Amazon fans that it's always worth looking on Amazon before making a bookstore purchase, because it's likely to be cheaper there than elsewhere. Those who subscribe to the Amazon Prime service don't even have to factor in delivery costs. The customer perception is that delivery is free, because Prime is a one-off annual charge.

Hence the rise of that accursed practice, showrooming. There are few bookstore staff who have not experienced the aggravation of helping a customer with an enquiry about a specific book, only to be told by the customer, "No thanks, I'll order it on Amazon when I get home. It's cheaper." Some customers even have the temerity to scan the QR code or barcode on the book proffered by the bookseller and order it online in front of their eyes, not realizing how offensive or tactless this is. Would the same customers go into a grocery store, ask the staff to find a particular brand of cereal, then tell them they'll order it elsewhere to save money? I don't think so—but somehow there seems a real ignorance among book buyers of exactly how the book trade works, as if somehow all retailers of all kinds are part of one big happy family with the publishers and the authors, all of whom will get their fair share of the takings at the end of the day out of one giant pot of money. Oh, if only...

Many traditional bookstore chains have started to offer online stores of their own, to help fight back against the onslaught of online specialists. Some offer the best of both worlds; for example, a click-and-collect service, grocery store style, so that customers may order their books and collect at their own convenience. Amazon also has collection points for those online customers for whom delivery to their door is not convenient or secure. Its new stores will also offer this service.

While the rise of the internet and the growth in popularity of online shopping has coincided with the decline and closure of many bookstores, it would be simplistic to jump to the conclusion that bookstores have been hounded out of business by the rise of online book retailers.

Firstly, a lot of high street and shopping mall mainstays have gone under, including many big names that the average consumer probably assumed were indestructible, even stores with enormous brand loyalty to which many consumers had a sentimental or nostalgic attachment. The threats to those stores are the same as the threats to bookstores: growing costs of trading (ever-increasing rents, rates, and staff wages), coupled with the increasing popularity of buying online.

Local population patterns change. For example, some formerly thriving city-center shopping areas have become ghost towns as out-of-town malls have grown up. On the plus side, other formerly derelict areas have been revived by redevelopment programs. For instance, many disused harbors and dock areas have been transformed into fashionable, desirable communities for the affluent, often including upmarket retail areas that may house new bookstores.

Even without the rise of the ebook, it is increasingly challenging for bookstores that stick with traditional trading practices to persuade customers to cross their threshold and part with their money.

Some chains have disappeared, most notably Borders. At one point, the US chain Borders seemed to be the exciting big chain, crossing the Atlantic to open up new-style stores in Europe, startling the old school with its fancy sofas and in-store coffee shops. But it closed in 2011, due largely, analysts say, to coming too late to online selling and ebooks.

All round the world, a large part of the highest-value, highest-margin segments of the business, such as hardback fiction, are steadily migrating to ebook and online fulfillment.

This does not mean that bookstores are doomed. "Books are not like recorded music," says Shaun Symonds, general manager of Nielsen Bookscan, and it is too often assumed that both industries are headed the same way. Research by PwC and others shows that, if anything, the total global market for books is growing.

Neither can we extrapolate from the closure of so many bookstores in recent years that the bookstore will soon be extinct. In some countries, the long, slow decline in numbers has either flattened out or turned around. In many countries, the number of stores is rising again, and there are good news stories, with a great many new indie entrants to the marketplace. While the slow decline of the once mighty US chain Barnes & Noble saddens book buyers and sellers everywhere, the American Booksellers Association recently reported a healthy growth in numbers of independent bookstores in the US, rising from 1,651 in 2009 to 2,094 in 2014.

This is encouraging, especially as it is happening in such a geographically vast territory, in which many occupants live too far from bookstores to be regular customers and therefore buy books online by default.

Global figures show that, if you adjust for the effects of the closure of major book chains such as Borders, there is, in fact, only one or two years of decline in sales volume over the past decade in most major markets. Every other year, including the most recent, the figures reflect a modest year-on-year growth in total books (including ebooks) sold on the year before.

Some businesses that have been floundering for years have turned themselves around and returned to profit, with heavily revised business models to suit modern market demands. The British chain Waterstones, once heading the same way as Barnes & Noble, recently reported its first profit for five years, after some major restructuring and rethinking.

Some chains have been extending their reach with new branches and ambitious expansion plans.

Equally, small independents have ridden the storm by rejigging their stock and expanding their offer with a careful selection of nonbook items, appealing events programs, and promotions. The highly successful US IndieBound campaign and the UK Booksellers' Association high-profile "Books Are My Bag" campaign are now annual fixtures on the booksellers' calendar. Small indie stores are also expert at ordering stock to match their specific clientele, whom they know and have chatted to in person, rather than just by analyzing ordering patterns in isolation.

While conventional bookstores know what sells through their own tills, few have customer data as detailed as Amazon's, and some don't even have a means of identifying and contacting customers for emailing purposes. Amazon's new stores will also be well placed to set up events and other services matched to each of its stores' local communities.

Bookseller Helene Hewett of The Anthology Bookstore, Cheltenham, braved the downward trend when she opened her first ever independent bookstore in 2015. She wanted to fulfill her childhood ambition after a previous successful career as a doctor.

"Running an independent bookstore these days is much more about being part of the community than just selling books," she says.

Her focus on building relationships with both local writers and readers is paying off. She is an enthusiastic host to the monthly authors group I run there, and every time I visit, the appreciation and loyalty of her local clientele is palpable. I witnessed her prescribe the best books to meet a gentleman's request for his grandchildren, before he turned to me to say completely spontaneously, "We are so lucky to have such a great service here for our community."

It's also worth noting that, in some respects, bookstores have valuable elements in their business model that many retailers would envy.

Firstly, there is generally a sale or return deal with publishers, which means that any books that do not sell after a set period of time can be returned to the supplier for full credit. Of course, most booksellers would rather sell the books than return them, because while they don't lose money by returning unsold books, nor do they make any. Every return means that they've had that part of a shelf tied up with a nonpaying lodger. It's also time-consuming to remove books from the shelves and package them up to return to the supplier, and not a little heartrending when you know their fate on return is likely to be forwarding to a cut-price remainder bookstore or even to a pulping plant, on the assumption that returned books, once they've been shipped, are no longer in sufficiently pristine condition to reissue to another bookstore. Often they do not even have to return the whole book, just the ripped off barcode or front cover, to prove it's not been sold.

Secondly, the book trade generally practices just-in-time delivery for books that are in stock at the publisher's warehouse. While self-published authors mostly avoid the need to hold inventory by using print-on-demand services, the business model of the Big Five and plenty of small publishers is still to print in large quantities. When customers order a book available from their usual distributor, bookstores usually receive next-day delivery, at a speed of service that matches Amazon's, but without charging the customer for postage. All the customer needs to do is call back into the store at their convenience to collect the purchase. With click-and-collect shopping gaining ground for everything from medicines to groceries, this service is a valuable asset for booksellers to be able to offer their customers, and one that's likely to gain more ground in the near future.

Bookstores Yet to Come

While it would be foolhardy to predict how many bookstores will be trading in five years' time, or ten or twenty, given current trends, it seems certain that, despite online traders' ambitions and successes, there will still be plenty of trading to be done—and enough to be worth any self-respecting self-publishing author's while to consider them a significant target as a means of connecting with the book-buying public. New players will enter, as Amazon has done recently with a handful of bookstores, playing to its own special strengths. Future bookstores are likely to be much more than bookselling zones, offering added value to the customer through a program of community events and services, meeting local social needs on a wider level. Whether or not it can be done at a profit is another matter, and in the chapter "Why Sell Self-Published Books through Bookstores Anyway?" we'll help you decide whether you should be targeting these bookstores with your books, before going on to equip you to do it as efficiently and cost-effectively as possible. But first, let's drill down a little further into the nature of bookstores, and of other stores that sell books without necessarily being dedicated bookstores, to help you choose which shops to target.

DIFFERENT TYPES OF BOOKSTORE

I t's all too easy, in our fervor to get our books into bookstores, to make insufficient allowance for their differences. This chapter outlines different types of bookstores and determines how best to approach each type.

Bookstore Chains

Obviously stores in big chains will have a different ethos from the small independents. Whether the chain is growing or shrinking, they will usually have strong corporate branding and company policies, although even that seems to be changing.

If I took you blindfolded into any branch of the British chain Waterstones, for example, as soon as you were unmasked, you'd know at a glance that you were in a Waterstones store, with its distinctive windowless rooms, black bookshelves and folksy shelf-edgers. Even though their geographical locations may be wildly different, once you've walked through the entrance, you're unmistakably on Planet Waterstones. My nearest branch, in an enclosed out-of-town shopping mall near Bristol, has a bland view of a walkway and other shop fronts, whereas the one I visited on holiday in Oban on the northwest coast of Scotland has a stunning harbor view at the starting point of a voyage to the Outer Hebrides.

Buying will be done centrally, and buying policy will be dictated centrally, but the stores would be less profitable and successful if they held exactly the same stock in every branch, regardless of the local demographic and geography. Even within a large chain, there will be some local variations, particularly in stock ordering. In the Oban store, for example, there is an abundance of books about Scottish interests and the Highlands and Islands, whereas in the Bristol store nearest me the local interest books are obviously all about Bristol. Yet their shared corporate identity is clear.

The same strategy that applies to the big grocery chains, where the differences are easier to spot, also applies to books: the same chain that stocks caviar and top-price champagne in an upmarket area will stock cheap white sliced bread and cut-price lager in a less well-to-do area.

The image of the bad corporate chain stores gobbling up brave little independents was crystallized in the 1998 Nora Ephron film *You've Got Mail*, in which the heroine, played by Meg Ryan, runs a venerable children's bookshop in Manhattan, a nurturing, warm-and-fuzzy, personal-services kind of place, while the tainted hero, played by Tom Hanks, is the lowbrow owner of a chain of superstores intent on putting her out of business.

Your stores are "big, impersonal, overstocked, and full of ignorant salespeople," she tells him, a sentiment you still hear widely stated in the book world. But actually large stores are making more risky and experimental fiction, more first novels, and more serious nonfiction available to general readers than ever before.

"The book business was an elitist, standoffish institution," Len Riggio told *BusinessWeek* in 1998. "I liberated it from that."

Riggio is the retailing entrepreneur who launched the Barnes & Noble superstore concept, with in-store coffee shops and spacious reading alcoves, that spread to Borders and Books-A-Million, and then to chains and independents the world over, turning the then rarified and elitist world of bookstores into recreational experiences.

"Riggio's critics have mocked his populist pose," says cultural commentator Brooke Allen, writing in *The Atlantic*, "but it should be taken seriously":

Before the appearance of the chains, a relatively highbrow, urban clientele shopped at the independents, and a relatively lowbrow, largely regional one bought mass-market titles at supermarkets, price clubs, and drugstores. Now, thanks to the chains and to internet sales, the vast territory between the two extremes has been bridged.

Elitists may carp, but the truth is that they are no longer quite so elite. These days shoppers in Buford, Georgia, and Rapid City, South Dakota, can pick up important titles such as Norman Cantor's Inventing the Middle Ages, Eugene Genovese's Roll, Jordan, Roll, and Andrew Motion's biography of John Keats—titles that are neither "popular" nor newly published—at their local Borders. (None of these books were available at the venerated independent Manhattan bookstores St Marks Bookshop and Three Lives, or at Los Angeles's hip and highbrow Book Soup, when I called.)

— BROOKE ALLEN

In the UK, Waterstones has added a new strand to its offering: stores that are individually designed to match the local vernacular, trading under a quasi-independent name, and designed to look as if they are one-off independents.

There is no real subterfuge. The Waterstones ownership is still clearly visible if you look for it, though there was a bit of an outcry by some who felt they'd been hoodwinked, but actually it's the same strategy that has worked very well in other sectors. For example, pub or restaurant chains that run to a precise, successful formula but with no two venues looking alike.

Lots of indie authors have said to me that they've been told by the local branch of a bookstore chain that it's company policy not to stock self-published books. They tell author friends the same thing, and before you know it, it's accepted as a universal truth. But that's an urban myth.

Bookstore chains can and do stock self-published books— provided they are approached in the right way and that they are convinced that your book will earn them money. (You'll find some inspiring case studies in the chapter "How I Do It".)

If you have approached a bookstore and been turned down with that line, it's very likely that either (a) the staff member is ignorant of the corporate policy, (b) they can tell at a glance that your book isn't viable for their store and they think this is the kindest way of rejecting you, or (c) you've really rubbed them up the wrong way and they don't want to deal with you under any circumstances. We'll come on to how to make a more effective approach in the chapter "How to Pitch Your Book to a Bookstore."

Independent Bookstores

Indie stores have much greater freedom to curate their stock in line with their own preferences and, most importantly, their customers'. Independent bookstores are likely to be smaller than the typical large chain bookstore. This means they have fewer staff and fewer customers, so they're more likely to build up personal relationships and better mutual understanding.

It's often the quirkiness of small indie shops and their projection of the owner's personality that makes them so alluring. Indeed, it would be hard to find any two independent bookstores that could be mistaken for being part of the same chain. For a whistle-stop tour indicating the enormous range to be found within the independent bookstore sector, check out Jen Campbell's *The Bookshop Book*, which profiles dozens of bookstores from all around the world, punctuated by interviews with famous authors talking about their fans.

Independent booksellers, like indie authors, relish their freedom and independence. They're often founded and staffed by people who have worked for the bookstore chains, so they are highly experienced. They find it refreshing to no longer have to adhere to corporate guidelines dictated from remote head offices with shareholders to please. What's not to love about a bookstore that offers a 10% discount to anyone with dreadlocks, or whose proprietor prescribes for each customer the appropriate tea from a long list on his café menu, as readily as he'll recommend a book? That's the wonderful Albion Beatnick in Oxford, England, which also bucks the trend by categorically not offering free WiFi for the benefit of customers.

"It's so analogue, it's anal," pronounces its website, which also emphasizes the store's participative community focus. "Help with the hoovering is always much appreciated," the website continues (that's vacuuming to non-British readers), and there's so much to love about its proud individuality that it's almost tempting to volunteer for that task.

Booksellers in independent stores are closer to the impact of the bottom line than employees in big stores. The proprietor of a small indie store not only depends on its success for a salary, but might also be using the family home to guarantee the business, and so stand to lose the house if the business folds. They are also responsible not just for keeping the store stocked and the customers happy, but for all the management tasks that would normally be shared between the large staff of a corporation: financial management and planning, tax returns, marketing, personnel management, property maintenance. Just as we self-published authors must take responsibility for the full job range of a publisher, the independent bookstore proprietor is CEO, personnel manager, finance officer, stock controller, and so on. Selling books to customers may be what drives the business, but it's a tiny part of what the proprietor actually does.

To be a successful independent bookseller, you have to be an entrepreneur, a multitasker, and an independent thinker. That makes them more open to negotiation than suited executives tucked away in remote corporate HQs. They are also more accessible—but that doesn't make them fair game to buttonhole at any time. Careful planning of your approach will improve your chances of success. We'll discuss strategies and tactics in future chapters.

Specialist Bookstores

The interests and constraints of bookstores, whether part of a chain or independent one-offs, will be dictated and constrained by two factors: their degree of specialism and their location.

Particularly if you're writing nonfiction, you should seek out any specialist bookstores for which your books would be a perfect match. For example, in the UK, Stamfords supplies travel-related books and maps, so if you've self-published a memoir of how you circumnavigated the world on a unicycle, it'll be an obvious target, because a greater proportion of space will be given over to travel-related books, and its customers shop there specifically because they're interested in travel. If you arrive in the store on your unicycle, you'll gain credibility and interest!

Specialist bookstores may cluster near relevant locations. Expect to find a medical bookstore on the campus of a medical school, or a legal bookstore near law courts and lawyers' chambers. They're worth seeking out if your book's the right match—but equally, you can save yourself some pain if you don't bother asking in a cookery specialist bookstore whether they'd like to take your latest zombie vampire novel.

Don't forget to check out secondhand bookstores, many of which also carry new books, aiming to get the best of both worlds by diversifying. Conversely, some bookstores that have previously sold only new stock now supplement their new book business with secondhand or rare book sections that can also operate online, bringing in another income stream.

Indie-Only Bookstores

One relatively new form of specialism is to stock only books published by small independent presses or self-published authors.

There are a number of retailers offering this service online, sometimes offshoots of organizations associated with indie authors, such as publishing services companies that have helped authors self-publish their books, or book accreditation and evaluation services.

There are also a handful of bricks-and-mortar bookstores that are attempting to do the same. This is a bold and interesting concept, because the average reader doesn't choose books on the basis of who publishes them, or whether they are self-published or trade-published. Most people, if challenged, would be unable to tell you the name of the publisher of the last book they read. Many wouldn't understand the difference between self- and trade-published, and fewer still would care about it. They're simply looking for good books produced to professional standards.

Buying indie isn't a political or socially conscious decision—it's not comparable to choosing to buy fair trade products or organically produced food, or clothing ethically produced without exploitation of child labor. If stores were to look for books that were produced at a living wage, most books would be ruled out altogether, including trade-published ones!

The success of such shops depends on careful curation plus the provision of an appealing customer experience to lure readers in. Florida bookstore PJ Boox (www.pjboox.com) has as one point of difference the strategy of displaying all its books face out, giving each author a floating wall shelf on which to showcase their books and offering the shopper an aesthetically pleasing and unusual shopping experience.

"A title on a spine from an unknown author isn't going to sell a book," says proprietor Patti Brassard Jefferson, an award-winning author and illustrator of children's books. "Readers are drawn in with the cover. We invite them to pick up and hold the book, and that makes a connection more comfortable." At the time of writing, her store's shelves host over 260 indie authors representing eleven countries, and she has plans to include 500 when at capacity. As well as scheduling author events, she facilitates interaction with featured authors who are too far away to visit in person via video chat options.

"Being able to connect authors and readers directly takes the entire book experience to a different level," says Patti. "Today's readers don't always want to be told what to read. They are discovering new authors of their own. We just make that quest easier."

As an indie author, you might feel that indie-only bookstores would be worth pursuing as a natural outlet for your self-published books. On the other hand, you might worry that their existence sets indie books apart from the trade-published ones, when it's more in our interest to gain parity for them and see them lined up on the same shelves together. You decide, because, hey, you're independent.

By the way, there are also online retailers offering indie-only books, which may sound appealing. However, the average reader will need a good reason to seek those out, rather than plumping for the websites of the bigger, general online retailers, or the website of their favorite bookstore. This is because readers are usually no more intent on buying only indie books than only books with blue covers or written only by authors whose names include the letter Z. What readers want is a good book, and the success or failure of any book-retailing enterprise depends upon the seller's ability to curate what the target readers want.

Unusual Bookstores

You find bookstores in the most surprising places. Fun photos of bookstores housed on rickshaws, tricycles, houseboats, and even donkeys abound on the internet. There are bookstores in converted chapels and churches, in disused barns and manor houses. Just about any building or vehicle can be adapted to house a bookstore, with the addition of shelves and a till. A quirky or romantic setting will add to the charm for the customer, though not always for the staff, who must try to provide efficient customer service without the benefits of modern technology or architecture. The nature of the location may impact their choice of stock and their capacity. There are only so many books you can fit on a donkey's panniers before it tips over, or into a barge before it sinks.

The bookseller in unusual retail premises must, therefore, be even more selective when curating stock. On the other hand, if the nature of the location makes it appealing to tourists rather than just to locals, it will have the potential to bring those books stocked to a wider audience than a conventional bookstore, including those who are not habitual book buyers or readers.

Nonbookstore Outlets

It's worth also considering whether your books would go down well in stores that are not bookstores at all. Many other kinds of stores choose to sell a limited range of books as part of a much more diverse product range. While this might seem a more obvious opportunity for nonfiction books (history books in relevant museums, travel books in tourist offices, etc.), it can also work well for fiction.

For example, US novelist Karen Myers' *Hounds of Annwn* fantasy series, which features a strong foxhunting theme, is stocked in equestrian and hunting equipment shops, and *Stocking Fillers*, my collection of short stories, whose cover is in the style of a vintage Christmas card, is sold in local gift shops among their Christmas gift range. I also target wedding gift stockists with my collection *Marry in Haste: 15 Short Stories of Dating, Love and Marriage*, the cover of which features a wedding cake.

Such arrangements are known in the trade as "special sales," and while these examples may seem like minor tangential diversions from the average author's marketing plan, they are potentially much more powerful. Led by executive director Brian Jud, the Association of Publishers for Special Sales (APSS) exists to help authors exploit the full power of such lateral thinking. On its website, it summarizes the publisher's (or indeed author–publisher's) dilemma as follows:

Publishers of all sizes are learning that limiting sales only to traditional channels may be the least effective and most costly way to sell books. This understanding has spawned a different way to market books, one that increases sales, revenue and profits for those who take their products to people where they buy, rather than waiting for consumers to come to them. That in essence is special-sales (non-bookstore, non-traditional) marketing.

Special-sales marketing is not a separate way of doing business. It is not even a new way of doing business. It is an integral part of overall marketing strategy, an extension of what you are probably already doing. If you are selling to bookstores now, you can sell to special markets without changing your habits or inventing new skills.

— ASSOCIATION OF PUBLISHERS FOR SPECIAL SALES

Special sales, says APSS, thus focuses not on selling through bookstores but through places "where your potential readers shop (bookstores, gift shops, catalogues), gather (seminars, libraries, associations) or work (offices, schools, hospitals)."

It may sound obvious that exploiting special-sales opportunities to the full requires building a presence in these places in a way that will attract potential readers to buy your books, but actually making that happen can be challenging. APSS aims "to help multi-format content publishers to increase their revenue and profits through sales to non-bookstore buyers," and it has impressive success stories to share, such as that of Amy Schoen. By thinking beyond the bookstore, she found opportunities to sell her book *Get it Right This Time*, about helping single people meet their lifelong partner, to cruise ship lines, to florists, and to online dating services for use as a premium to attract new business.

APSS is a membership organization offering extensive resources and benefits in return for a modest annual fee. Find out more at its website at community.bookapss.org. It's also an excellent source of ideas and inspiration.

Which to Choose?

Given the array of stores outlined above, which should you choose to target?

For the time-pressed indie author, focusing on large chains where book-buying is centralized might seem a more efficient use of time than schlepping round to individual indies. However, you are then pitching yourself against a much bigger field of competition, including big publishers with a proven track record in sales, and money to spend on securing prime store space. (Yes, those high-profile tables and specialized displays aren't there because of the bookstores' generosity—more about that in the chapter "How Bookstores Operate".)

You may get lucky, and you may have a standout book that will leap out from the ton of books that arrives in the buyers' offices each day. Or you may not. The most you have to lose by trying is the cost of a book and the time it takes you to prepare your covering material and submit it. But usually you'll have a better chance of gaining attention from central buyers if you've already scored some impressive successes in your home territory, both in independent bookstores and in local branches of your targeted chain.

There's a lot to be said for targeting those stores on your home territory. Being a local author adds an extra reason for them to stock your book. Local stores may be in your comfort zone, making you feel more confident, especially if they're shops that you frequent as a customer. Traveling to stores costs time and money. Target too many distant shops and your potential profit will quickly be guzzled up by your travel costs. Few of us can expect to be able to walk to many stockists, though I do know at least one author who, living in a town blessed with several bookstores, takes pleasure in cycling round them at weekends to replenish stocks.

When I say target local stores, I don't just mean local independent bookstores, because local branches of chains may also prove receptive, if you go about it in the right way with a suitable book—but more about that in the chapters "How to Make Your Book Bookstore Ready" and "How to Pitch Your Book to a Bookstore".

But first, before we look in more detail at how to approach your chosen stores, let's consider whether and why you really want to invest the time, effort, and money into getting your books into bookstores of any kind, or whether you'd be happiest to stick with selling online—which is most indie authors' starting point—and devote time that could be spent on marketing elsewhere, marketing other formats, or writing more books.

WHY SELL SELF-PUBLISHED BOOKS THROUGH BOOKSTORES ANYWAY?

Before you take the time and trouble to decide which bookstore to target, be sure you really want to get your books into bookstores. Why should you bother when plenty of indie authors, including some hugely successful and high-profile ones, ignore the sector, content with their online sales success?

Having already established their books and a following via online retailers, they are happy to stay in their groove of write, publish, repeat, as they watch their sales snowball. Many don't even stray beyond what is most people's entry point into self-publishing these days: publishing ebooks via KDP (Kindle Direct Publishing) to be sold through Amazon. As other ebook distribution platforms grow and gradually take market share from Amazon, most authors broaden their reach to Kobo, Nook, iBooks, and so on, but others stick strictly with Kindle. Although a few bookstores promote ebooks in-store, if you're ebook only, by definition, you are out of the running for getting your books stocked on physical bookshelves. Robin Cutler, Director of IngramSpark, makes a clear case for including print in your catalog.

Despite the publishing prophecies from five or so years ago claiming that readers were moving in mass to their ebook devices, we now know that in 2016 and into the foreseeable future, the printed book continues to dominate the market as the preferred format for reading. The truth turned out to be that a huge number of people still prefer the experience of turning pages, browsing shelves of titles and carting around a reading device that hasn't changed much in the 1500 years since bound pages replaced the scrolls of antiquity.

As it turns out, there are some genres such as romance and thrillers where many readers prefer their content served up effortlessly and often for free to their iPad, Kindle or Kobo. But even now the most ardent advocates for digital publishing from a few years back are now suggesting that a multi-format strategy may be the best approach for indie authors today.

I have recommended for years that it's best for authors to make their content available in as many formats, and as widely available, as they can afford. With a publishing industry that is changing so rapidly, there is no way to predict an audience for your book or even know where and how readers prefer to purchase. With platforms such as IngramSpark that combine distribution directly with ebook and print-on-demand technology, this strategy is fairly easy and inexpensive to realize.

— ROBIN CUTLER, INGRAMSPARK

Many authors who prefer to focus on ebooks therefore still produce paperbacks so as to have something to "show and tell" at events, and to share with people who don't believe that books exist unless they see them in print, or who think ebooks don't count as actual books. These authors often produce their paperbacks on CreateSpace and/or IngramSpark, or commission a small private print run. They might not bother with their own ISBNs, using their provider's free ISBNs, if available, to keep the process as simple as possible.

(Whoever owns a book's ISBN is deemed its publisher—more about the implications of ISBN choices in the chapter "How to Make Your Book Bookstore Ready".)

But at least with a small stock at home for hand-selling and print-on-demand books available to order online, they don't miss out entirely on print sale opportunities.

Why Limit Yourself to Ebooks?

The reasons these authors cite for sticking to ebook only include:

- less time-consuming
- more profitable per book (typically 70% of selling price for Amazon ebooks priced $1.99–9.99)
- cheaper production costs—just a front cover jpeg and digital text, rather than a full wraparound cover with formatted interior
- no delivery costs
- frees up more time for writing more books and marketing the back catalog
- current customer base for ebooks provides adequate income
- anticipated sales of paperbacks would not generate sufficient profit to cover the additional production and marketing costs.

Print generally has a much narrower potential for profit than ebooks. Selling paperbacks as well as ebooks online is almost always more profitable. This is because by selling your books through a bookstore, not only do you have to cover the production costs of the print edition, you're introducing an intermediary with more substantial overheads than an online store: rent, staff, taxes, heating, lighting, advertising, etc.

Clearly these overheads have to be paid for, and that's why bookstores expect to receive a substantial discount on books they buy to sell on. Most booksellers will expect 35–45% from your recommended retail price, and even more for books for which they promise to provide extra sales focus, for example 60% for books sold in high-volume outlets such as airport bookstores. They are also open to negotiation for extra fees in return for high-profile positions, such as face up on tables toward the front of the store.

The Benefits of Bookstore Selling

Provided that you go into the prospect of selling through bookstores with realistic financial expectations—i.e. you may not make much profit or sell many copies—there are sound reasons for pursuing this path. Some of these are practical issues:

- Certain books are much harder to sell in digital format, in particular children's books, as younger readers still prefer to read print books.
- Very complex technical books full of diagrams, charts, photos, and other illustrations don't translate well into digital format.

There are also more emotional reasons for wanting to sell your books via bookstores:

- validation of your status as an author (in the same way that many successful indie authors would also be happy to accept a trade publishing contract, on the right terms, to indicate to themselves that they've really arrived as an author)
- personal love of bookstores as cultural centers in our society that makes having your book stocked there seem particularly desirable
- a love of physical books
- loyalty to specific bookstores where you are a regular customer

- a lifelong ambition to see your book on sale in a bookstore, formed long before ebooks and online book retailers took off, hard to shake off despite the book-retailing revolution that we've witnessed since the turn of the twenty-first century.

Piers Alexander, the historical novelist who kicked off our #Authors4Bookstores campaign, described on the ALLi blog his lasting passion for bookstores as the driving force behind his decision to focus the launch of his debut novel on a print edition with high production values with which to target bookstores.

Although it made his self-publishing process more complex and higher risk, as a serial entrepreneur he was happy to rise to the challenge:

I grew up in Luxembourg, and the best bit of visiting England as a kid was coming to bookstores with a sweaty pawful of pocket money. Booksellers are nice, thoughtful, helpful people, and their lives have become a lot more difficult in the age of the internet and book discounting. Even so, I frequently find them going out of their way to place books that they personally like, that they think their customers will like, rather than just going with the obvious bestsellers. When I decided to publish The Bitter Trade *independently, I was very keen to get good reach through bookstores.*

The thing is, I like "proper books". I like holding them, infusing them with my own peculiar musk, and then passing them on to unsuspecting friends. And in an age when millions of writers are desperately trying to game the Amazon system, when quite ruthless email marketing companies drive everyone towards 99 cent ebook promotions, I love the fact that people pay good money for good books and find them in good bookstores. So I decided to print them in the old-fashioned way, which is a bit of a commitment.

Going from 100 to 500 paperbacks halves the cost of production. Going to 2,000 plus halves it again—and you can't do that on

CreateSpace. That means it's an all-or-nothing thing. I'm pleased to say that I broke even within seven months... until we print the next batch. Which is bigger! Ladies and gentlemen, don't try this at home. Stock control is a nightmare.

And here's what happened: I've sold copies to I think about 10% of the UK's high street bookstores and libraries through the lovely people at Gardners, one of the UK's leading distributors. That's very cool. Even cooler is that the fiction buyer for WHSmith—who just loves historical novels—agreed to take a consignment for all their airport shops, and the book went into the charts...

The best thing I ever did was to invest properly in print. I had a dream of seeing The Bitter Trade in airports. My ex-agent thought of it as a literary novel, but I have always seen it as commercial. So I produced it in trade paperback format, took a deep breath and spent even more embossing and using spot UV (varnish) on the front cover—and cursed myself for a fool right up until the moment Matt Bates from WHS said that he liked the jacket, loved the story and could see it in his stores.

And by the way, most trade publishers have to pay a lot of money to get into the Airport Exclusives spots. I just had to print the books. I guess there's another lesson here: don't listen to people all the time. When it comes to the really big decisions, go with your gut.

— PIERS ALEXANDER

Piers's strategy and determination were rewarded, but clearly also brought with them serious responsibilities and cost implications that are not to be taken lightly.

Scottish novelist Anne Stormont is another author whose love of bookstores dates back to her childhood:

I loved bookstores when I was little. My granny was the one who would take me and she would buy me books as an occasional treat. I still love them—the independents, the chains, the ones with coffee shops, galleries or gift shops attached—love them all. And although I do read in both ebook and paper format, I still prefer a proper paper book. I publish in both formats and I ask bookstores to stock my books. Long live the real books and long live the book shops.

— ANNE STORMONT

These may be emotional reasons, but that doesn't invalidate them, especially when they are followed through with sound business decisions, as in the case of both authors quoted above.

Note the absence of one significant reason: to get rich. If it's the fast track to clear profit you're after, selling your books via bookstores is not the obvious route. For a start, you'll have to invest far more heavily to make your book bookstore ready than simply to sell it online in ebook form. We'll talk more about that in the chapter "How to Make Your Book Bookstore Ready."

But for all kinds of books, if you've invested the time and effort into producing a print book for hand-selling and promotional purposes, you might as well explore all retail opportunities, rather than just those to be found online. It would seem a shame not to at least investigate possibilities and options, so that you can make an informed decision about what would be in your own best interests.

If you're still reading this far, I'm assuming you've decided that you do want to try to get your books into bookstores, so the next step is to gain an understanding of exactly how bookstores operate, so that you can devise a campaign that will help you mesh with their practices and thus gain a greater chance of success.

HOW BOOKSTORES OPERATE

This chapter provides broad guidelines on how bookstores operate, but each country's system is a little different, so please do further research into your local territory's way of working before finalizing your decisions. The simplest way to clarify the finer details that apply to your own country is to befriend your local bookstore staff and ask them—and of course to follow appropriate publishing news sites and blogs, including ALLi's.

Wherever you are based, the best way to understand how a bookstore operates is to try to see it from the other side of the counter. Most authors have no idea what it's like unless they've served time at some point in their career as a bookseller. Those who have develop a lasting respect, such as MC Beaton.

There's no shame in not instinctively understanding how bookstores work. How can you be expected to know unless you've had firsthand experience? The important thing is to learn about it now, so that you don't blow your chances from the outset. Once you're able to put yourself in the bookseller's shoes and see the self-published author's pitch through the bookseller's eyes, you'll be able to make a more effective and efficient pitch for your book.

A Cautionary Tale

Every bookseller in every store is likely at some point to have had a clumsy and inappropriate approach from the indie author from hell, which may have skewed their perspective of self-published books and their authors. Let's picture the scene.

On a busy, crowded Saturday, when customers are queuing at the tills, Fred Fly walks into the bookstore, straight from the door, with no real interest in any aspect of the store other than its potential to stock his book. Although he lives less than a mile away, he hasn't been in the shop since he was a schoolboy, so has to search to find the sales counter.

He joins the small queue, sighing impatiently as the lady in front of him pays for a large pile of expensive books using her well-worn store loyalty card. When he finally gains the bookseller's attention, he produces his book with a flourish, almost as if expecting a round of applause.

"I've written a book," he says, pointing proudly to his name. "That's me, Fred Fly, and I live across town from here. So I'm a local author. And I've self-published it too. So, how many copies would you like me to provide for your first order? Ten? Twenty? Fifty? I have a gross of them out in my car, so if you want to display a big pile in your window, I have plenty of stock."

The bookseller looks at the book, trying to work out what genre it's in, and what the local connection is. He also has trouble reading the title, which is in an artistic swirly print in dazzling colors. He flips it over to read the blurb, in hope of the missing clues. It's full of anonymous reviews—or rather, gushing quotes attributed to an anonymous "Amazon reviewer."

The bookseller's hackles rise: only this morning another potential customer, after grilling him for information about the best birdwatcher's handbook, had turned down the chance to buy the recommended book, saying "Oh, no thanks, now I know what I'm looking for, I'll order it on Amazon when I get home—it'll be much cheaper and save me carrying it."

The bookseller is conscious of the growing queue behind Fred Fly, and though he doesn't want to waste genuine customers' time, he doesn't wish to appear rude. After all, his store has a reputation to maintain.

"Can you just leave your AI sheet with me please, so I can look at it later?" Fred Fly looks blank. "You know, with the salient points about the book? What's special about it? Price? Stockists? Reviews? Endorsements?"

Fred Fly frowns.

"What do you need some sheet for? I'm giving you the whole book for free. Just try reading it, and I'm sure you're going to love it. All my friends do. My mother said it's the best book she's ever read."

"What about your terms? Are you offering sale or return? What discount can you offer? We expect 40% as standard."

"Forty per cent discount? After all my hard work writing it? Are you trying to be funny? No, thank you, I'll take it elsewhere, to someone who really appreciates a good book when they see it."

Exit Fred Fly, in a huff, never to darken the store's doorstep again, much to the bookseller's relief. Back at home, Fred tweets his disgust at the lack of support for self-published books from his local bookstore, tagging the store in case the bookseller sees the error of his ways and decides to order his book after all. Meanwhile the bookseller discreetly shares his experience with colleagues in a private forum, garnering sympathy and moral support and putting them on their guard for when Fred comes knocking at their bookstore door…

I'm sure no one savvy enough to read this book would ever be as crass as Fred Fly, but this fictitious case study is a fun way to illustrate the difference between the author's perspective and the bookseller's. (I should add, as in my novels, any similarity to any real person, place, or event is purely coincidental!)

An Extreme Case

Fred Fly's example is not the worst we've come across in ALLi. Just recently a bookseller's Facebook thread told of a woman who had come into his store expecting him to accept two boxes of her newly self-published autobiography for sale. She had no prior relationship with the bookstore or the bookseller, and no obvious claim to fame that might generate demand for her memoirs.

The bookseller's heart sank even further when she produced a sample book from the box: it wasn't even a book, but a spiral bound photocopy of her typescript, run off in vast quantities by the local copy shop.

"If she'd ever been inside my bookstore, or any other bookstore, and taken a look at what was on the shelves, she'd have seen for herself that this was not the sort of thing we would ever sell," said the exasperated bookseller.

Other bookseller friends were quick to condemn this as a classic case of a naive author who had not bothered to research her market or learn the rules of the game, and at the same time cursed all self-published authors by association.

Luckily for her, this particular bookseller was kindhearted and patient enough to offer sympathy and to direct her to ALLi for guidance on how to self-publish more effectively. Such incidents, as well as being personally distressing for the would-be author, are not helpful to the cause of self-publishing, because displaying the lowest common denominator tarnishes the sector as a whole.

I was quick to point out on the thread that this incident was hardly representative of the sector, and that there were plenty of self-published books produced to such professional standards that they were indistinguishable from trade-published titles. Fortunately, this particular bookseller already knew this, having had many good experiences of self-published books, and noted that his current bestseller was an indie title.

This cautionary tale may seem far-fetched, but just about every bookseller has a similar horror story to tell about an inappropriate approach with an unsaleable book. If you ever feel that a bookseller is reacting less than enthusiastically to your approach, try to view your approach through their eyes.

Fred Fly may have paid a visit just before you did, putting the bookseller off self-publishing until their faith is restored by a better prospect. Make sure you are that prospect by understanding how bookstores operate so that you can get your pitch right.

The Bookseller's Objectives

Whereas the author's objective is to get books stocked in a local bookstore for reasons of their own, such as validation or ambition, the bookseller's objective is far more practical: to run a successful bookstore. Your book is a tiny piece in the jigsaw of the business, and it may not even fit at all.

What makes a successful bookstore?

- attractive premises, well maintained, in a good position
- a carefully curated mix of the right books to appeal to the local clientele
- effective stock management to ensure the most profitable use of shelf space
- efficient service to customers by motivated, happy and well-informed staff
- strong administration and financial management skills.

What threatens a bookstore's success?

- books that won't appeal to its customer base (staff will have a very clear idea of its customers' likes and dislikes)
- books that don't sell but clutter up shelves that might earn more money with different stock
- books that are substandard, e.g. full of errors or which fall

apart, damaging customer goodwill and potentially driving
them to shop elsewhere
- people who disrespect or waste staff time, preventing them
from dealing with customers waiting to be served
- unprofitable deals, e.g. profit margins that do not cover the
cost of sale.

To agree to stock a book, the bookseller must believe that it is:

- produced to professional standards, in terms of writing and
production values
- a good match for the clientele
- offering a realistic profit margin, i.e. discount against its
recommended selling price
- easy to source, ideally via the normal distributor, with new
stock fast to arrive.

When you pitch your book to a bookseller, those are the
considerations that will be top of their mind. Even if you are a
longstanding customer, know the staff well, and buy books there all
the time, if your book doesn't meet those last criteria, you're unlikely
to get a good reception. If you're lucky, the bookseller will let you
down gently, say encouraging things about your book, and encourage
you to keep writing. If you're not so lucky, and especially if you're a
stranger to the shop, you may get less sympathetic treatment,
especially if there is a queue of customers behind you, waiting to pay
for their purchases.

The Competition

But take heart, because trade-published books have to run the same
gauntlet as you. You are all making a bid for a place on the shelf
alongside other players in the industry, as if your books are
participants in a vast balloon debate. It's down to you to make the case
for your books not to be jettisoned.

You may think bookstores can carry a lot of stock, and a first glance at the figures suggest you're right: 20,000 in the case of a city-center store that I frequent. But think again: there are currently over 25,000,000 print book titles listed on Amazon.com. A bookstore may thus stock less than 0.1% of them—or only one in every 1,250 books that are in print.

Clearly there is only room for so many books in a bookstore, and those that are there have to pay their way. Like tenants of bookshelf space, they must sell enough copies to justify the replenishment of their stock. If a book sits on a shelf without selling any copies it's dead space, earning the bookseller a nil return, and will quickly be removed from the shelf by any bookseller wishing to stay in business. The tenant who never pays any rent should expect eviction.

Actually, it's worse than a nil return—because removing books that don't sell creates an admin load. That said, at least the bookseller doesn't have to bear the cost of the stock that hasn't sold: they purchase their stock on a sale or return basis, so that the publisher refunds them for any books that are returned unsold, provided the publisher has guaranteed a full refund on unsold books. (We'll discuss the sale or return policy from the indie author's perspective in the chapter "Financial Considerations".)

The size of this workload is made even greater by the average shelf life of a book. Even those that sell well initially may grind to a halt after a few weeks, once launch publicity dies down, and are quietly dispatched when the demand slows or stops. It's easy to think of bookshelves as static objects, but in reality they're more like revolving doors. To stock a book for any length of time, long or short, the bookseller has to be convinced that it will earn its right to shelf space.

How Booksellers Buy Books

So the obvious next question is: how do booksellers choose their stock? Like any other retailer, they carefully choose and curate their product range to best please their target customers. No one knows a store's customers as well as the booksellers who work there, and each store will hold different stock. Even in a chain, where book-buying is done centrally, the buyers will take into consideration the target audience of each store and stock it accordingly, rather than sending out the same stock to every branch. Centralized chains may or may not give a certain degree of autonomy to local managers, on the basis of their local knowledge.

Where are booksellers **most** likely to find out about new books?

- trade publications (*Publishers Weekly* in the US, *The Bookseller* in the UK)
- national press (*The New York Times*, *USA Today*, *The Times*, *The Guardian*, etc.)
- regional and local press
- social media
- bookseller friends and colleagues (most booksellers will have many friends in the trade)
- publishers.

All of these will carry a certain amount of authority, a kind of third-party approval that will help build the bookseller's confidence that a certain book is a safe bet to stock. The publisher is the only one who makes a human pitch to the bookseller, in the form of sales representatives who contact or visit booksellers directly to promote their latest batch of books. These reps are largely professional, knowledgeable, slick—and respectful of the bookseller's workload.

"I just had a rep in here who pitched me for his publisher's top 100 titles of this season with just 10 seconds per book," a bookseller once told me, appreciative of the efficient use of his time.

It is possible to buy the services of an independent rep for your self-published book, but you'll have to sell a lot of books to justify the cost. If buying distribution services, you need to note that there are two kinds on offer:

- full-service distribution, in which a rep makes in-store visits and actually sells your books to booksellers

- wholesale distribution, which makes your books available through the distributor's catalog, but doesn't includes the services of a rep to sell them.

To be clear, CreateSpace, IngramSpark and Lightning Source offer wholesale distribution as standard, i.e. your books will be listed passively in their catalog. Further services are available as an extra chargeable option.

Full-service distribution is what most indies want but can't afford. You need a certain level of sales to support it and to be successful already. There's a reason for traditional publishers to be so slow and long term with publishing and promoting books: to justify full-service sales.

— ROBIN CUTLER, DIRECTOR OF INGRAMSPARK

Robin Cutler recommends past sales of about 50,000 books as the entry level to justify the cost of full-service distribution. It also requires your commitment to offering sale or return.

It's also worth noting that books actively "pushed" in this way, rather than ordered spontaneously by the bookstore, are more likely to be returned unsold. Robin Cutler estimates an average 60% return rate. Gulp.

To have your books featured alongside trade-published books, sold by a dedicated and specialist in-house team directly into bookstores of all kinds, sounds extremely attractive, but the economics of print-on-demand publishing probably won't allow for full-service distribution unless your book is in a high-pricing genre or you are established as a consistent bestseller.

Even if you are confident of attracting sufficient sales, you'll also need to be prepared to fit in with the conventional timing of the way trade-published books are sold to bookstores, i.e. up to six months in advance of a book's publication date. There may be other criteria to meet, such as being required to supply a large number of printed copies up front, so there is ready-made stock to sell, thus guaranteeing promised delivery times to buyers, which might not be possible via print-on-demand.

Should you wish to take this route, there are at least two services available for indie authors:

- Ingram Publisher Services (US)
- Matador Star (UK and Ireland)

To use either of these services, your books must be published via Ingram or Matador respectively.

Be sure to read all of the details before making a commitment—and be wary of any company offering full-service distribution at a surprisingly low cost. Lesser companies have been known to sell the service without following it through, simply warehousing your stock instead of actively selling it to bookstores.

In such a competitive industry, where so many publishers compete for shelf space for their protégés, it's also in publishers' interests to build good long-term relationships with booksellers, in hope of always getting a good reception for their brand. The same bookseller I mentioned before made me smile when he told me his response to an unsolicited phone call from a publisher's rep:

"What can we do to help your bookstore sell more books?" asked the rep.

"Get rid of me, for a start," quipped the self-deprecating bookseller.

Although booksellers will be targeted directly by the agents of publishers, they generally don't order books from the publisher, but through a preferred distributor or wholesaler. This simplifies paperwork—a single invoice and a single delivery for a whole raft of books from multiple publishers. It also makes life simpler for the publishers, because the costs of consolidated shipments can be shared.

Conspicuous by its absence from the list above is the author. That's because booksellers don't usually deal—or want to deal—with authors individually, unless those authors have been invited to do a book-signing or other event in-store. We indie authors may believe that no one is as powerful an advocate as we are for our books, but sending individual authors to pitch for their books, with one-off invoices and deliveries, is really anathema to a system built around consolidation, to the benefit of all parties.

"Here in India, we notice that most retailers do not want to register yet another account, and thus want to go through one of the established distributors," reports Ritesh Kala. "It makes it that much easier to get the books stocked."

Whether or not you promote your self-published books to booksellers via the services of a rep, it is essential to your success that your book looks fit to display in a bookstore, and the next chapter will help you ensure that your books truly are bookstore ready.

HOW TO MAKE YOUR BOOK BOOKSTORE READY

A devout man who has fallen on hard times prays to his god. "Please, God, I've been a faithful servant. I've been good to my family, worked hard in my job, and helped my neighbor and my community. Would it be so hard for you to make it possible for me to win the lottery?" God's reply: "My son, if you want to win the lottery, it helps if you buy a ticket."

Is your book bookstore ready? It may seem to be stating the obvious, but a surprising number of self-published books fall at the first hurdle by simply not being up to the professional standards demanded by bookstores. Most booksellers have been approached by hopeful indie authors clutching books that have been far from market ready. Sometimes they don't even have a physical book to show the bookseller, unlike the trade publisher's rep, who will have ARCs (advance review copies) issued pre-publication to entice the support of stockists and reviewers. To expect them to take on a self-published book is challenging enough, but to get them to commit to a book they've never seen is beyond optimistic.

Booksellers also complain of being shown books that simply are not fit to be seen in a bookstore, whether because the cover is unprofessional or inappropriate for the genre, the layout inside is unprofessional, or the price is not viable in a bookstore setting. No matter how wonderful the content is (an obvious point to add to your checklist!), if it's not presented right—and by right I mean in a way that will make readers buy it—the bookseller won't be interested. Such behavior also puts the bookseller in a very difficult position and creates barriers for your future relationship.

So help yourself. When your book is up against stiff competition from millions of others for a space on any bookstore shelf, it makes sense to ensure your book is bookstore ready before casting it into the ring.

That means it should pass muster as if it were a professionally trade-published book. Yes, we know that self-published books can be better than trade-published ones, pushing the boundaries of convention and commercialism, refusing to be constrained by genre, and so on—but that doesn't mean we may flout any of the professional standards that big publishers set, in terms not only of the writing, but also the many other elements that are the responsibility of the self-publishing author: editing, proofreading, formatting, cover design, title, and blurb.

Does Your Book Pass the Identity Parade Test?

This test may seem anathema to staunch indie authors, fiercely protective and proud of their indie status, but I strongly advise you to submit to it. If you put your book on a display table in a bookstore among those published by big publishing companies, would it blend in? Would it fit on the shelves, the same size as other books in its genre? Would it recognizably belong in an obvious niche? If it's a fluffy romance, is it in light and airy colors, trade paperback size? If it's horror, is its cover suitably foreboding?

Are you sure you're aiming at the right niche for the content of your book? Or even more than one niche? Novelist Rohan Quine has executed a remarkable coup in having his cross-genre novels stocked in a flagship store, by convincing them that it was appropriate in fantasy/sci-fi, literary fiction, and horror.

If your book falls outside of any standard genre, booksellers, like publishers, won't know what to do with it or where to display it to ensure interested readers might find it. This doesn't mean that you need to blindly follow what everyone else is doing. After all, you are an indie, and the freedom to play things how you wish is one of the great joys of your status. But if you're going to be wildly different, expect a harder sell to the bookseller, and don't be surprised if your book is rejected as unshelvable. It's your prerogative to be as different as you like, but just be aware of the implications.

Author and poet Dan Holloway, whose more conventional thriller had been given prominent displays in his local chain, did not expect to get the same treatment for *Evie and Guy*, his experimental novel written entirely in numbers. Not getting stocked in a bookstore was not going to deflect him from his creative intentions.

If your book is very different from trade publishing norms, perhaps that's a sign that bookstore distribution is not for you. Of course, there's always the exception to the rule, with the book that is so radically different that, while there is no obvious place for a bookstore to display it, it leaps off the shelves and becomes a groundbreaking bestseller, the leader of the pack. Surely there was once the first adult coloring book that furrowed the brows of booksellers everywhere, before those brave enough to stock it found it quickly boosted their profits. Early adopters were ahead of the pack in setting aside not just shelf space but whole areas of their stores to showcase the fast-growing range, especially in the run-up to the season of festive gift buying. I confess I am a fan, and although I probably have enough coloring books in my house now to have some over to take with me to my grave, it doesn't stop me taking a look at that section whenever I'm in a bookstore that has addressed that genre.

Thanks to shoppers like me, the mushrooming popularity of adult coloring books made a major contribution to bookstore takings last year, as *Fifty Shades of Gray* (no coloring pun intended) did the year before that. Most likely another curiosity will be along each year to take up the mantle of the maverick that made good. But the vast majority of books sold in bookstores will look like, well, books sold in bookstores.

How to Avoid Rookie Errors

You may write, design, and present your book to match the norms in your target genre, but does it meet professional standards? Or would it jump out from the crowd shouting "Self-published! Home-made! Cover flung together on Word!" You know the answer I'm looking for…

Too many books give away their origins by making simple mistakes that would never appear on a trade-published book, such as adding "BY" before the author's name, or even "Mr/Mrs/Ms" (yes, I've seen them all), or by using inappropriate fonts on the cover for the type of book. Comic Sans for a historical novel? It's been known to happen.

Other rookie errors include forewords or acknowledgments sections that read like a bad Oscar acceptance speech. Keep those short and functional. Do not thank everyone you know, or mention what a trial and a triumph it has been to write your first book, or the fact that you've published it yourself because no one else would. Do not add a PS asking readers to email you when they find errors. You may think all those things, but if you need to say them, put them elsewhere, such as in reader newsletters, where your target booksellers won't see them and take them as an indicator of your amateurism. Ask yourself: what would {insert name of your most idolized professional author here} do?

Fortunately, such basic mistakes happen less often these days. We're by no means taking all the credit for this, but since ALLi was founded in 2012, the standards of self-published books do seem to have risen, partly as indie authors becomes better informed, more sophisticated and more experienced, and as rank amateurs drop out of the game due to failure. But there are still a large number of self-published books that DO look self-published, which tarnish the rest by association. Make sure yours does not fall into that trap.

Does It Match the Needs of the Store?

Assuming that your book looks a perfect fit for a standard bookstore genre, and is written and produced to professional standards, you still need to ask yourself whether it's a good match for the bookstores you wish to target. Booksellers curate their stock to suit their local market, and they know their clientele better than you ever will. A book that is a perfect fit at one branch on the east coast of the States, for example, may be a nonstarter on the west coast. This is particularly true for small independent stores, where purchasing decisions are made at local level, rather than by a remote head office. (By the way, do not discount the wisdom of the head office on account of its geographical distance—its buyers have vast amounts of very accurate data about local purchasing patterns, gathered via loyalty cards and research both within their stores and elsewhere, at their disposal.)

In most cases, we'd recommend that the first bookstores you target should be those on your home turf, where you should ideally already be a familiar face and a known customer. (If not, it's time you started shopping local.) That way you can build your confidence and experience before taking your book further afield.

Should you wish to dive into chain bookstores with centralized purchasing, you will be unlikely to be able to make that pitch in person. Instead, you'll need to target the appropriate person by email and post. If so, do your research first to obtain the right name for the buyer of books in your genre. In large genres, there may be more than one. Bear in mind that the competition for attention of central purchasers will be much greater than at a local store, so your pitch will need to be even more carefully prepared. Phone the head office and grill the receptionist to get the name of the most appropriate person.

Even where there is centralized buying, if you are able to chat up a local member of staff, you may gain an introduction to the appropriate central buyer, and even a recommendation. Branch staff also talk to each other, so if your book does well in one branch, you may find orders coming in from other stores following their recommendations.

Do You Have a Plausible Publisher's Imprint—and Do You Need One?

One of the questions often discussed among indie authors seeking bookstore listings is whether you should publish your book under an imprint—that is a publishing company's name—rather than your own. One school of thought says that presenting your book this way adds weight by looking more professional and conventional. The other argument protests that you should wear your book's self-published status with pride, declaring yourself to be proudly author and publisher, unadorned.

As with so much in the indie publishing sector, the decision is entirely up to you—whatever you feel comfortable with. You must, of course, comply with any local trading and taxation regulations in your own country. In some regions, it's simple and straightforward to assume a trading name, while actually trading as an individual; in others it's more complex.

If you do decide to take the imprint route, make sure before choosing your imprint that it's not already taken by someone else, that it sounds like a proper and professional company, and that it's appropriate to the books you'll be publishing. Naming your imprint Fluffy after your cat will detract from the impact of horror titles. Think long term when picking your name—if you're likely to publish across a wide range of genres, don't restrict yourself by choosing a single-genre name. Vampire Press may be fine for your fantasy thrillers, but won't look so great on the spine of your new range of cookery books.

Do You Have Your Own ISBNs?

Related to the question of imprints is the issue of ISBNs. ISBNs are internationally recognized book identifiers, each unique to a particular book. One part of the ISBN identifies the registered publisher of the book, while another indicates the specific book. ISBNs are issued by a single supplier in each country, for a set price. In some countries they are issued free of charge. When you order your supply of ISBNs, you specify the name of the publisher at the point of ordering. ISBNs are not transferable.

The value of an ISBN becomes clear when you realize that it is the key that unlocks all the information a bookstore will require about any book. If a customer can provide your ISBN, the bookseller will be able to identify your book, even if the customer can't remember the correct title, spell the author name, or describe what the cover looks like.

This is great stuff, of course. But there are occasions when it can work against you. For example, if you have published your print book solely via Amazon's CreateSpace, using the ISBN supplied free of charge, when booksellers look up your book's ISBN they will instantly see Amazon listed as your publisher.

This immediately creates barriers to buying. Many booksellers will, as a matter of principle, refuse to stock books bearing the CreateSpace imprint because they perceive the company to be a threat to their viability.

Secondly, even if they are not averse to stocking it on principle, they may be unable to order it via their usual distributors. Yes, anyone may order it from Amazon's website, but that would be at the retail price, bypassing any chance of a profit margin.

Many newcomers to self-publishing see the ISBN as an avoidable cost when you are able to obtain them free of charge from CreateSpace, not realizing the implications for bookstores, but ALLi strongly recommends you buy your own, so that you or your chosen imprint is registered as the publisher of record.

There is only one ISBN supplier per country, and you must buy your ISBNs from your country of residence at whatever rate they dictate. Lucky you if your national government subsidizes ISBN costs, as some do to encourage cultural development, or even issues them free.

ALLi recommends that you produce your print books simultaneously through IngramSpark and CreateSpace, using the same ISBN, which should be one bought and registered by you under your own author name or imprint, whichever you've decided to use. That way, when a bookseller searches for your ISBN, you will show up as the publisher, not CreateSpace. You also avoid your book being listed as out of stock on Amazon when there are no IngramSpark copies in the warehouse. This out-of-stock message usually errs on the side of caution, suggesting it may be weeks before your book is available, or even that it is not known when or whether it will be back in stock, deterring orders from customers used to prompt delivery. This may be unhelpful to authors, but it's a sobering reminder that Amazon's priority is to provide a satisfactory experience for customers (and thus to boost its earnings) rather than to help authors reach readers.

There are several detailed blog posts in the ALLi Author Advice Centre that give more details on this important subject. Just type "CreateSpace Ingram" in the search box to pull up the latest ones.

Once you've published your books using your own ISBNs, there's a second stage to attend to: adding a summary description of the book to the central ISBN records. In the UK, this is done at Nielsen. You will have to sign up for a (free) account for yourself as a publisher at www.nielsentitleeditor.com. If you are not in the UK, check with your ISBN provider. Obviously you will have information about your books elsewhere online, but this is an essential starting point for outlets in the supply chain to populate their own records, so make sure you complete it. It's pretty straightforward.

How to Price Your Books

No matter how perfect your print book looks, if its price is inappropriate, bookstores will shy away from stocking it. Too expensive compared with similar books in its genre and it won't look competitive; too cheap and there'll be no room for a decent margin for the bookstore (or for you). Pricing print books is harder than pricing ebooks because they cost more to supply, for obvious reasons: materials and production cost much more than a digital file, and they also cost more to transport. The larger your book, the more challenging it will be to make it profitable. If printing any part of the interior in color, your choice of standard or premium color production needs to be carefully considered to keep the sales price viable.

Fortunately, distributors like Lightning Source, IngramSpark and CreateSpace make the task easier by providing a ready reckoner to help you adjust your price and tweak your discounts to suit your financial requirements, and so provide a safety net against loss. It's also prudent not to print your retail price on your cover, in case you decide to raise or lower it at a later date. Bookstores will be able to gather your price when they scan the barcode on your book, and they'll most likely handprice it with a label-printing gun so that their customers know the price before they buy.

When you set your discounts with the distributors, you get to choose from a preset range. Usually 30% is the minimum, because that's what you need to get a listing on Amazon and Barnes & Noble, but most bookstores expect at least 40%, and the top rate is an eyewatering 55%.

Bear in mind that these rates don't mean the remaining 70%/60%/45% is all yours. The distributor will also charge you the production cost, of course, so your own margin will actually be much lower. Take heart, though, that it's still likely to be far more than the 5% that you'd typically earn from a publishing contract with one of the Big Five.

Also note that the discount is what is offered to the wholesaler, not the bookstore. The wholesaler will take its service fee out of that discount, and the remainder of the discount is what goes to the bookstore. The more players there are in the distribution chain, the less the bookstore will get—although the discount will always be what you determined in the first place.

On a more cheerful note, you will be paid when the wholesaler pays, and not when the book is eventually bought by the end user—the bookstore customer.

How to Prove You'll Be Driving Customers In

Bestselling American thriller writer Diane Capri is sanguine about the issue of getting books into bookstores: "To me, the big issue is not so much getting the books onto shelves, but getting them from the shelf into the buyer's shopping bag and out the door. That's where the real challenge lies. If we could come up with a workable answer to that one, my guess is the booksellers would be glad to stock the books."

Therefore, use every resource that you can to demonstrate to your target bookstore that your book will be in demand. Share great reviews, press cuttings, news of public events, past and present. One neat and accessible way to do this is via the advance information (AI) sheet, a regular tool of the trade for publishers' reps, providing an at-a-glance summary of the key selling points of a book in a single A4 sheet.

How to Create Advance Information Sheets

It's standard practice in the publishing trade to produce what's usually referred to as an AI in the run-up to a new book's launch, either on its own, or with a free ARC of the book. Whether or not you choose to offer a free sample of the book (and you should do that only if you're sure one is wanted, so as to avoid waste), it's definitely worth producing an AI sheet for a self-published book.

They're just as useful for indie authors as for big publishers. Why should we operate any differently, when there is this tried-and-trusted formula for effective communication with reviewers and booksellers?

The AI sheet is a single sheet of A4 paper, printed one-sided, ideally in color, but sometimes mono for the sake of economy. The AI sheet has three main uses:

- to entice early reviewers to agree to read and review a book (the actual book may then be sent only to those who agree in advance to review it)
- to accompany ARCs, making it super-easy for reviewers to include the correct information in any reviews they write up
- to encourage and enable booksellers to place orders easily by providing a persuasive sales pitch coupled with practical details of how to order.

As well as being distributed to reviewers and booksellers, AI sheets may also be made available as downloads from the press and publicity sections of publishers' websites. This enables any potential reviewer or stockist to print off one for their own use at any time. As an indie, make sure you put yours on your website too.

The typical AI sheet includes a cover image, title, and author name, plus a brief overview of a book, an author bio, some testimonials, and technical data (ISBN, price, launch date, formats, etc.), plus contact details in case of query. You may also include an author photo as an optional extra. Not all publishers do, but for the indie author, I think adding a photo is a great idea, as it's more likely to be you taking your book into the store. It's also a great way of helping booksellers remember you and put the right face to the right name, further down the line.

Try to echo the style and font of your book on its AI sheet, at least for headlines and images, so that the two are a recognizable pair. Keep the body copy in a common serif font, though, such as Times New Roman or Garamond, to make the information easy to read once it's caught the reviewer or bookseller's eye.

All this information is presented in an orderly, logical manner to provide an at-a-glance summary of the features and benefits of a new book, in an attractive yet familiar and digestible form that busy reviewers and booksellers can absorb quickly and accurately.

Offering an AI sheet also adds credibility to self-published books and small indie press imprints. Providing one to a prospective bookseller or reviewer is a clear indication that we understand how they operate and that we will be easy to work with. It shows we speak the bookseller's language. It shows we respect reviewers' time and needs.

Unlike so many other marketing materials, AI sheets cost next to nothing to produce and distribute. You can knock one up on your own computer, print it off on your home or office printer, and add it to your own author website, or, if you publish under an imprint, on that imprint's website—or both. If you have a page for each of your books on your author website, it's a matter of moments to add a download of the AI sheet as a clickable option.

Maintain Momentum

While the AI sheet may help you get your book stocked, you need to do all you can to get it to shift off the shelves once it's there, to encourage a repeat buying pattern.

Make sure you tell local people where your book is to be found. Include the address on leaflets and other promotional material, as appropriate. Consider running an event with the store. Think about ways in which you can collaborate with the store to create sales.

Less effective tactics, such as authors surreptitiously rearranging shelves where their books are stocked, are common. In *The Bookshop Book*, Jen Campbell quotes Ian Rankin saying, "You can always tell when you're traveling which authors have been through the airport bookstores before you, because their books are the ones facing out on all the shelves."

Even cheekier, and hardly effective, are those authors who secretly plant their own books in stores while no one's looking, in the hope that someone will want to buy it, take it to the till, where the bookseller will fail to find it on their stock list, wonder why, when it's clearly in demand, and formally place an order for more.

If cheeky is your tune, use that productively and don't overstep the mark and alienate customers or booksellers. Too many indie authors trying too hard, or disrespecting people's time and attention, is one of the reasons that many bookstores now treat self-published authors with caution.

This applies to fellow and sister authors too, as thriller writer Alison Morton reports:

I've been door-stepped in bookstores by inexpert indies. One even followed me round my local chain store, demanding I should buy his book "in solidarity." Bleating and whinging doesn't work.

— ALISON MORTON

Take the time to think out a strategy that will work and implement it.

Is It Easy to Buy in and Maintain Stock?

So now all the bookseller has to do is keep buying in more books—easy, right? Or is it?

To make sure that it's feasible and practical for the bookseller to maintain stocks of your book, the simplest solution is to make it available to order via the bookseller's usual distributor, so that buying your book will just be one extra line on the regular bulk order and invoice, rather than requiring a separate invoice just for your book. As I mentioned earlier, raising paperwork, dealing with invoices, and paying bills all costs the bookseller time and money.

It may be a helpful analogy to compare this task with your own buying practices, such as your weekly grocery shop. In the twenty-first century, most people buy the majority of their groceries from one store, and pay for it all at the till with a single card payment. Yes, we complain about waiting at the checkout, but think how much harder it would be if, for every item, you had to pay at a separate till, in a separate transaction. Or, if certain items were never available from the supermarket, but had to be obtained from a separate small shop round the corner. It wouldn't take much to persuade you, time-pressed as you are, to forget the smaller shops and just field a substitute that was available in the supermarket.

Yes, there are plenty of shoppers who still favor small indie shops and farmers' markets, but that's not the point. If you want to maximize your sales in bookstores, you need to make life easy for the way booksellers buy in. "But what about the likes of PJ Boox?" you may think, remembering the innovative indie-only store mentioned in an earlier chapter. PJ Boox has a different business model, charging authors rental for shelf space.

Making your books available via the usual established distributor assures booksellers that new stock will arrive quickly, so that they don't have to keep any customers waiting. It also looks professional —as if you're a part of the core trade, rather than a market stallholder standing hopefully on the periphery of the supermarket car park.

Next question: how do you make your book available via the distributor? Two ways, is the answer—either by becoming a regular supplier to the distributor and managing stock yourself (that's the hard way, requiring you to be able to dispatch just-in-time deliveries all year round), or by publishing your book through a distribution platform that deals directly with the wholesalers. The most significant of these are Lightning Source and IngramSpark, the latter a subsidiary of the former. Lightning Source is designed to service small to large publishing companies, and IngramSpark is more geared up to the single indie author or very small publishing firm. These services also allow you to specify your discount rates for each geographical territory, so that bookstores will know without having to ask you whether your rates suit them.

Now, before we move on to financial considerations, let's recap on how to make that all-important pitch to your chosen bookstore with a handy checklist in the chapter "How to Pitch Your Book to a Bookstore".

Remember, most bookstores list their indie bookselling policies on their websites. Before you make a sales call, familiarize yourself with the way they do business and make sure you're OK with those policies.

For example, many indie bookstores have a consignment policy, which means they'll stock your book, but they will only pay you if and when it sells. Some stores, such as Left Bank Books in St Louis, Missouri, have a reading fee. This fee compensates the staff for the time it takes to read your book, discuss it with each other, and make an evaluation of whether it's appropriate for their shelves.

If this, or any other policy, is not agreeable to you, don't try to talk them out of it. It's their store, their policy, and their financial model, and they get to make the rules.

"When submitting your book for review," says Mark Tiedemann of Left Bank Books, "have a realistic attitude." That means waiting patiently for the staff to read and evaluate your book—and respecting their decision. If your book is rejected, don't talk trash about the store. Other bookstores in the area will find out, and they will be worried about what you may be saying about them.

HOW TO PITCH YOUR BOOK TO A BOOKSTORE

D rawing on all that you've read here so far, you now need to summon up all your courage, optimism, and determination and go for it. Here's a step-by-step guide to help you walk through the process like you've been doing it all your life...

Assemble Your Ammunition

It's show and tell time! Along with a pristine copy of your book, pack up your AI sheet to provide an at-a-glance summary of all the key data about your book, plus any marketing collateral: local media coverage, early reviews, and endorsements from respected authors in your field... Anything that will serve as objective proof of its worth as a saleable, profit-making resource in any bookstore.

Prepare Your Questions in Advance

Think of all the questions a bookstore buyer might ask you, and have your Q&A ready prepared in your head. Why should the store stock your book? Where should your book sit on the shelves—which genre? Is there a local connection? Is there any recent or planned local or national PR that will alert people to look out for it? What online presence do you have? Will your author website promote this store as a stockist? What about your social media? Do you have any events planned? Are you interested in holding an in-store event—and if so, would you bring your own audience? The better you have prepared possible questions in advance, the more confident and competent you will be in-store.

Choose Your Target

Start with the shop that makes you feel most confident of success: the one at which you are a regular customer, or the one whose clientele is the best match for your book. Once you've found success in one, you'll have more confidence to approach another, so be kind to yourself and pick off the easiest target first.

Pinpoint the Most Appropriate Staff Member

Phone the store, check out its website, or ask at a preliminary visit for the name of the staff member who is responsible for buying in stock. That way you can go straight to the person who has the most power to say yes to your proposition—and you won't embarrass yourself by giving your full pitch to someone who is only there for the day as cover for someone off sick, or who is about to move to a new job in a different store the next day.

Make an Appointment in Advance of Your Visit

Yes, you may get lucky and find that your target person is on the till if you pitch up at the store unannounced—but on the other hand, they will be there on duty to serve customers, and may not have the time to spare or the inclination to chat to authors who turn up unannounced. And if they're happy to make an appointment, it shows they're already open to the idea of buying your book, so you can go into the meeting feeling you're already off to a good start.

Have a Dummy Run

Be your own mystery shopper. If you're not already familiar with the bookstore, visit it beforehand, familiarize yourself with its layout, its opening hours, its website, its event program, and its typical customers. That way you'll be able to speak more knowledgeably and convincingly about why your book is a good fit for this particular store. Your research may even give you ideas for your meeting: for example, a proposal based on the success of a recent event held there.

Act the Part

Before you set foot in the store for your appointment, mentally prepare yourself to behave appropriately: be polite, professional, pleasant, and respectful. Stand tall and put your shoulders back—it'll relax you and make you feel and look more confident. Adopt a genuine smile, as if you're pleased to be there and to meet your contact (well, you are, aren't you?). Be ready to shake hands, or exchange bows, or whatever other gesture is the body language of the business-like in your country.

Offer Evidence

Accompany your elevator pitch for your book with evidence that it's not just you and your mother who think it's wonderful: flourish that ammunition you so carefully prepared before you came. You've probably got used to it by now, but when you show it all at once to fresh eyes, it will be impressive.

Be Passionate but Practical

No one can be as passionate about a book as its author, nor as knowledgeable, and you're in a unique position to answer questions about it. But make sure you listen to your contact's questions and respond to them, rather than treating the meeting as an opportunity to perform a soliloquy. Try to view the book from your potential stockist's perspective, and answer any questions, which are more likely to be about the practicalities of processing orders than about what inspired you to write the book in the first place. And if you are asked that kind of question, take heart—it's a buying signal! You've convinced your contact it's worth giving your book shelf space, so now you can concentrate on overcoming any obstacles to sealing the deal—sale or return arrangements, discounts, payment methods, and the like.

Follow the Buyer's Lead

If the buyer says yes, fantastic! Make sure you then go on to fulfill the agreed obligations, delivering the agreed number of books (if they're buying direct from you rather than from your distributor), promptly collecting unsold copies if you've agreed on sale or return, and submitting paperwork efficiently as required. Then move on to target your next most likely store.

Don't expect your buyer to take a whole case of your books straight away though. Most buyers will test the water with a small number of copies—think low single figures—and come back for more if those sell. So don't be disappointed. Have faith in your book—and try to hasten those first sales by promoting the store as a new stockist, via your website, social media, etc.

If the buyer doesn't make an immediate decision, accept that they need more time and ask what the next step should be—should you phone or email, or call in at a certain time, or leave it to them to contact you? Don't apply pressure or be at all ungracious. At least they haven't given you an outright no, and that's a good thing! Any reasons for hesitating are likely to be sound and considered. They may want to consult colleagues, to consider how it might fit in with other books ordered in that genre, or even to take the time to read the book in person. Wait until the agreed time to follow up your meeting, and when you do so, do it courteously by the agreed method, such as email rather than phone.

And if the buyer does say no, at least they've given you the chance to pitch. Accept defeat graciously. Try to assess whether there was anything you did wrong, or whether it's simply the case that the book isn't a good fit for the store, and once you've gleaned anything there is to learn from the experience, move on. There are plenty more bookstores out there, and at least now you have a ready-made contact for when you're ready to go in and pitch your next book.

Whatever you do, don't take rejection personally. Remember there are so many books out there vying for the same shelf space as you in that store, and only a tiny percentage can physically fit. The buyers who curate that stock are experienced, specialist professionals, and they make their decisions for sound commercial reasons. It's disappointing, of course, if you're a longstanding regular customer of a particular bookstore that refuses to stock your book. If it's any consolation, the buyer probably feels bad about making that decision, but, at the end of the day, they have their job to do, and their objectives are different to yours.

Say Thank You

Finally, whatever the outcome, thank your contact for their time and consideration, and make sure you have left contact details for future reference (these should be in your AI sheet, but you may also want to leave a card or bookmark if you have one), and leave promptly. Lingering in the shop afterwards to browse or even buy a book would be courteous and wise.

The Numbers Game

Assuming that in theory you can be successful in getting a potential bookstore to stock your books, in the next chapter we'll look at the financial considerations surrounding your deal.

FINANCIAL CONSIDERATIONS

The next logical question is whether the economics make sense. Is it worthwhile for both you as the supplier and for the bookstore as the customer interface to stock and sell your book?

Is It Potentially Profitable for the Bookseller?

Let's recap: you've got a book that is beautifully written, professionally presented, and a great fit for the clientele of the bookstore that you are targeting. Sounds good enough? Think again. Unless you're able to offer booksellers a viable profit margin, they may still turn you down. Remember, there are plenty of other books, authors, and publishers vying for the same shelf space. If they offer a better business proposition than you do, you may still fail to win over the bookseller. It has to be not only worth the bookseller's while to stock it, but be as valuable a contributor to profit as the best contenders.

A classic newbie error is to neglect to include in your calculations a substantial profit margin for the bookseller. Some authors seem outraged that the bookseller wants to take a slice of the pie at all. Why does the bookseller need a cut of your retail price? It's called capitalism, and that's how it works. Why do booksellers need such a high percentage? Just look at the issue from the other side of the till: book margins are the oxygen of any bookstore business. Booksellers stray from these established margins at the peril of their store's viability. Just think of your book as a tenant in the shop, having to pay its rent and other overheads: its share of the lighting, heating, staff wages, and so on, all of which are effectively the running costs of its little space on the shelf.

When you look at it that way, the bookstore's cut seems less of an imposition and more of a bargain. I often wonder at the care booksellers put into selling each book for such a tiny amount, and how they stay in business—and stay cheerful—at all.

The industry standard bare minimum a bookseller will expect is 30%, but 35–40% is more usual, while big chains offering prime spots in multiple stores may ask as much as 60%. For self-published authors operating on a print-on-demand basis, in which the print cost per book is higher than traditional offset litho, such a high percentage can be difficult to accommodate without making a loss. This dilemma is often the determining factor for indies when deciding to turn their backs on bookstore sales.

It's down to you and your negotiating skills to decide exactly what hit you're prepared to take on your book. Some authors are so keen to get their books on the bookstore shelf that they'll accept orders on a breakeven basis, or even at a loss. But you are not obliged to give the bookseller more than you wish to. You can walk away from any deal.

If you are one of those who wishes to get your books stocked at any cost, will it favor you to offer a higher discount? There's no firm answer there—it depends on the nature of your book. If it's appealing to a clear niche market in which you have little competition, the value of your book to the bookseller is higher than if you are writing in a large genre along with many other authors. If the bookseller can feed the same demand with books at 40% or 50% or 60%, they'll need to have a very good reason to stock your book at a lower profit.

However, if you're able to convince the bookseller that your book, at a 30% margin, will sell three times as many as one with the same retail price at 60% profit, you have an advantage. It's not rocket science; it's simple arithmetic.

If booksellers won't take your low-margin book as part of standard stock, they may still be prepared to order it for customers who ask for it—a response to the "pull" of the customers, rather than their own "push" to sell it. Booksellers aim to please their customers and pride themselves on going the extra mile. I spoke to a bookseller recently who was placing special orders for books that would earn her literally a penny profit, because she valued that customer and regarded it as a special service. Let's hope the customer appreciates her dedication to duty and buys plenty more books at a high margin to repay the bookseller's kindness. But bear in mind that, when you're asking for a lower margin, you're really asking for your books to be subsidized by the books that are selling at a higher markup.

When setting the discount, it's easy to assume that the bookseller gets the whole of that amount. The situation is more complicated than that. Andy Bromley of IngramSpark explains:

This really isn't specific to POD, it is part of the global supply chain of books. This is the same with litho printing because it isn't the printing format but the difference between the retail discount and wholesale discount. It's complex because the wholesaler who supplies the bookstore may buy from another wholesaler. Discount is agreed between the retailer and wholesaler on a contractual basis and there are variables that come into play that determine the discounts (volume, location, size, negotiation skills). Large multinational publishers might have their own distribution chain because they have critical mass, which is why they can beat indies (economy of scale is 95% of it).

— ANDY BROMLEY, INGRAMSPARK

It's not possible for the indie author (or any other kind of publisher) to know exactly which bookstore gets what, because these amounts are individual and private contracts involving the distributor, wholesaler, and bookseller. But it is clear that the setup is more complex than it seems at first glance.

Not all booksellers can negotiate the same deals with publishers, distributors, or wholesalers. Some big chains of bookstores have much more buying power than others, simply because they can shift books in much higher numbers.

The way the marketplace operates varies around the world. Ritesh Kala describes the scenario in India:

The discount received by bookstores mainly is the result of their own negotiation power. The large chains can get a discount as high as 40–50%, whereas the small independents are happy with 25–30%. The other issue is that not every small store can buy directly from the large distributors, so they are supplied by other subdistributors who keep a margin in there as well. However, the overall discount received by bookstores is always dependent on the discount offered by the publisher to the main distributor. The large ones can give the same distributor about 10% lower discount as compared to the smaller publishers, and still reach many more bookstores.

— RITESH KALA

That bigger markup may make the difference between ordering and not ordering your book. The author, incidentally, gets the same compensation or royalty however a bookstore orders your book.

So, although you may be offering 40%, for example, by the time the other parties have been involved in the chain, the bookstore may receive only about 20%. Fundamentally, although the situation may look simple to you, the author, when you set your discount in the different territories, the true situation can be more complex, with slices of that discount divided up between whatever distributors, subdistributors, or wholesalers there are in the chain. Theoretically, from both the author's and the bookstore's perspective, the more direct the better—although the bookstores presumably accept the reduced discount as a trade-off for other helpful benefits from their distributor or wholesaler, such as being able to order books from multiple authors and multiple publishers on a single invoice, and practical concessions such as free delivery and collection, and favorable payment terms.

Therefore, no matter how you feel about offering a discount, don't rush to accuse any bookseller of greed, because they may be getting far less than you assume. In any case, it's up to you to set the discount, and no bookstore or distributor can extract from you more discount than you are prepared to allow. You just need to bear in mind that the more generous a discount you allow, the more attractive your book will be—though if it's a book that a bookseller doesn't expect to be able to sell in the store, even 100% discount isn't going to be an attractive option. If the book doesn't sell, the profit will be zero, and the bookseller would be better off having a profit-generating book in that space on the shelf.

Clearly the fewer parties involved in the transaction, the more profit for both the indie author and the bookseller, with the proviso that the bookseller prefers to deal with multiple authors via one distributor. Distributors also usually offer a key benefit that the sole trader indie author would be unable to offer: free delivery, even for an order of a single book.

Publishing via IngramSpark or Lightning Source enables indie authors to get books into bookstores via the main distributors, because Ingram has an established relationship as their supplier. This is one of many reasons we recommend indie authors to publish with IngramSpark.

However, it doesn't solve the issue of diminishing profits when more parties are involved in the distribution chain.

Ingram's service, ipage, is an attempt to cut out the middle-men. It enables bookstores to order any books from its catalogue directly, for speedy, free delivery, on all orders of any size. None of the books in the catalogue are identified as self-published, which is also helpful.

ipage is being rolled out globally and in any of the growing number of territories in which it is operational (currently US, Canada and UK with Australia next on the list) any indie author who has published via either Lightning Source or IngramSpark may set up a free ipage account.

If you do this, your print-on-demand books will always be shown as in stock and available to booksellers, and will always be promptly despatched, with 48 hours as the target timescale for paperback titles.

Bookstores need to have an ipage account for this to work. In the US and Canada, where booksellers tend to be more familiar with Ingram, many have been quick to embrace this new service. In territories where Ingram is less well known, a bookstore may need to be persuaded to deal with an additional distributor to their usual choice.

In return, they will almost always earn a bigger discount by ordering an indie book via ipage than via any other distribution route.

If you suspect you're dealing with a bookstore that hasn't yet become acquainted with ipage, do explain it to them. They may assume the only way to order your author-published books is in small consignments and may well thank you for the introduction, as they have much to gain from it.

You'll find more information about ipage at: ingramcontent.com/ipage.

Are You Offering Sale or Return?

Besides speed of delivery and ease of ordering, another significant concern for the bookseller is whether or not you are offering sale or return. To spell out exactly what this means, if you tick the box to offer sale or return, it means that a bookstore may effectively order copies of your book speculatively, without a commitment to selling them. Thus, if your book doesn't sell after a set period, the bookstore may return it to the supplier for a full refund, leaving you to cover the production cost without the sale to offset it.

Think long and hard before ticking that box. While you may think that you would be happy to write off the cost of an occasional return, if it guaranteed bookstore shelf space for your book, doing so exposes you to much greater risk. Just supposing you pulled off a particularly good piece of marketing, leading to increased awareness of your book nationwide, or one of your blog posts or tweets went viral—there could be a surge in demand from bookstores whose radar you'd suddenly appeared on.

There could feasibly be hundreds or thousands of orders, but without any guarantee of sales. If the marketing hubbub dies down very quickly, most or all of the books ordered at its peak might be returned unsold, leaving you responsible for a massive debt. Small publishing houses have gone out of business this way.

Novelist Chris Longmuir reports on her near miss with sale or return:

One thing I have learned to look out for is the sale or return policy expected by booksellers. I was caught once when Foyles wanted to return books they had ordered for Crimefest (literary event). However, I was able to bodyswerve that one because I had given no such agreement. It did alert me to the problem though, because the markup on paperback books is minimal after the discount and postage is applied, and if returns require to be financed I would be seriously out of pocket. All my invoices now have a statement at the bottom saying "All sales final: No sale or return policy", and so far it has worked.

— CHRIS LONGMUIR

If having their stock underwritten seems to give bookstores an unfair advantage over the individual author, that's too bad—the system is designed to sustain viable bookstores, not to balance authors' bank accounts.

But do not despair: as mentioned earlier, deciding not to play the sale or return game won't necessarily eliminate you from any bookstore interest. Bookstores will almost always buy in a book to fulfill a specific customer order, even if it's not on sale or return, because they have effectively already sold the book, therefore there won't be a return.

By the way, it's worth noting that, if you have approached a bookstore in person to try to place your books, the bookseller may not realize that your books will be available via the standard distributors, so do go out of your way to make that clear to them when making your pitch. Although obviously you should always respect the bookseller's experience and knowledge, they are not infallible or all-knowing, so if you're sure of your ground, be prepared to gently inform or politely correct a bookseller if need be.

When novelist Rosalind Minett was told adamantly by small local bookstores that they could not accept her books, she says

---

"I just phoned Ingrams, who confirmed that the little bookstores who would only take copies from me, not order, were mistaken. Ingrams DO distribute through Gardners every day, also Bertrams and Askews."

— ROSALIND MINETT

Remember, for the vast majority of booksellers, the bulk of their business is not done directly with the author, or with the self-publishing sector, so they are still on a learning curve. Take the opportunity to help ease them along that curve, but only when it really is appropriate and you're sure of your facts.

The Personal Touch

Even when your books can be provided easily through the normal channels, booksellers may sometimes seem to prefer to deal with the author direct, as I've found myself when placing my books in my nearest stockists. If that's what they prefer, consider whether it's better to go with the flow, even though by this point you may realize it's much more convenient and cost-effective for you to have your books part of that consolidated order and shipment rather than visiting regularly to replenish their stocks or collect returns (if you choose to do so). Incidentally, if you're supplying directly by hand, offering sale or return is less risky, because you know the potential number of returns is small, and that the returned stock will be in better condition—possibly resaleable—than if submitted via delivery drivers or postal services.

Thriller writer Anne Stormont reports:

"I've had a similar experience in local bookstores in Scotland: they want me to provide the copies directly, even though they're available through their usual distributor as I went with Ingram Spark."

— Anne Stormont

It may be simply an economic consideration, if the bookseller buys via a wholesaler who is taking their own cut of the discount first. Thus, the bookseller will make more per book if buying directly from you at the discount you'd offer via your distributor, even when adding in to the equation the value of the extra time and trouble it takes to process your invoice and payment.

You might decide that hand delivery has other unexpected benefits, such as opportunities to build strong relationships with the booksellers, the chance to chat to customers, and regular occasions to remind the bookseller of your existence and to update them with your news. English novelist Hattie Holden Edmonds told me that it's one of her favorite times of the week when she cycles around her stockists in her hometown of Whitstable on the Kentish coast to take in new stock. While not all of us have the luxury of being able to maintain supplies without the need for petrol, parking, or postage costs, her attitude is inspiring.

Why, then, don't booksellers want to buy all indie books directly from the authors? The time required to deal with separate individuals for each book may be one factor, but also the booksellers may be getting other benefits from the distributor, such as free postage for delivery and returns, or prolonged payment terms, such as 60 or 90 days credit, and the ability to stock a book at a strategic time to suit their customers rather than timed around your visits. "But generally, the more direct you can deal with booksellers the better," says Andy Bromley, who also reports at the time of writing some exciting new plans to make it easier for indie authors to distribute their books direct to booksellers around the world via IngramSpark.

The Bottom Line—Is It Profitable for You?

In the final analysis, the economics of selling your books through bookstores are complex, and partly outside of the author–publisher's control. As the author, you must pay great attention to setting your side of the bargain, with careful consideration of selling prices, discounts, and terms and conditions (especially sale or return). Many authors decide the prospect of selling through bookstores is so fraught with complexity, risk, and dubious profitability that the game is not worth the candle. On the other hand, those who reject the option are effectively cutting themselves off from any potential readers who dislike ordering online and prefer to order through their local bookstores, whether for moral or ethical reasons, or because they are technophobes.

If having read this far you've decided that selling your books through bookstores simply would not repay the time, effort, and costs, even if it does cut you off from a certain sector of potential readers, it's up to you to make the decision not to pursue that route. As ever with indie publishing, you call the shots, and whatever decision feels right to you is the right decision for you. Don't let anyone tell you otherwise.

But you do not need to give up on bookstores entirely, because there are other ways of selling your books through bookstores, which may be more profitable and desirable, and which you should not dismiss without due consideration. In the chapter "Other Ways of Selling Books In-Store" we'll describe these other possibilities.

OTHER WAYS OF SELLING BOOKS IN-STORE

E ven when a bookstore is unwilling to order your books to stock and sell in the conventional manner, that doesn't mean it won't ever sell your books. If you're organizing or taking part in an in-store event, it's possible to use the consignment system.

This means your books are stocked at the store during that event, and possibly shortly before and shortly afterwards, and sold through their tills. Customers won't notice any difference, and the store will still receive the agreed profit margin, but no distributor or wholesaler is involved.

Consignment deals are negotiated in advance at a local level between you and the store management. You take in an agreed number of books, they add them to their stock for the duration of your event, and you take away the unsold ones afterwards, which they remove from their stock.

You then invoice the store for the books it has sold on your behalf, at the agreed discount. In effect, it will have stocked your books for a day.

While that may seem less satisfactory than having them in stock for longer, if you manage your event well and demonstrate strong demand and interest on the day, the store management may be persuaded to stock your books long term. And if it doesn't, well, at least you've had a glorious day of being the star of the bookstore, which, with strategic use of good event photography, you can use to generate further useful PR via your website and social media.

Book Launches

Holding an in-store launch is a great way to celebrate the birth of your book. However, do not expect the bookstore staff to run it for you. You will need to treat it as your own party, at your own expense, providing the refreshments, decorations, advance publicity, and invitations to ensure you have plenty of guests show up.

Even if the bookstore kindly advertises the event for you, don't expect it to field many guests from the general public. That will be down to you. To help raise your credibility and build your long-term relationship with the store staff, do all you can to bring in everyone you know. Even better, see if you can persuade them all to buy books on the night, via the store, especially if you know they're likely to buy them anyway.

A good launch, well run, can be exhausting and expensive. Don't expect to recover your costs in profits from your book sales. But do be on the lookout to extract every benefit you can from the event, from sharing advance publicity on your website, in the local media, and on social media, to post-event news stories.

Some bookstores prefer to run events outside of their normal opening hours so as not to interfere with trading patterns or sales of the rest of their stock. In stores that have very little room to move, they may even prefer to host events at a different venue away from the shop, though endorsing it from the shop and promoting it as their event. Don't be offended if they suggest either of these alternatives; just graciously accept what you're offered and make the best of it.

Novelist Sandy Osborne offers an encouraging case study of the launch of her debut novel *Girl Cop* at her local store:

Organizing a launch isn't dissimilar to planning a wedding. Invitations, wine, glasses hire, helium balloons (color coded to match the cover), photographer, and flowers for a special guest.

I even managed to persuade the manager to let me have a window display—positioning a full-sized model of me, in uniform, outside the shop, along with numerous posters/copies of the cover and a small table with a few books displayed on it.

I sent out invites to everyone I know. As the launch was going to be after Christmas, every Christmas card I sent included an invite! I recruited four friends to "meet and greet" and run the bar. I handed out fliers to everyone I thought looked within my readership, from the checkout ladies in the supermarket to those queuing behind me! I looked out my old Dr Marten boots from the attic and organized my table display for the night.

I texted and emailed everyone in my contacts lists both before Christmas and again shortly before the event. I didn't ask for RSVPs—I just crossed my fingers! I also managed to get a piece in the local paper.

Over 180 people turned out to help me celebrate its final release on a cold January evening—and I sold over 100 books!

— SANDY OSBORNE

While a strong launch clearly requires hard work, and is more likely to cost you money than turn a profit, it's a great way to impress bookstore staff, as well as to bolster your own ego and local status as a successful author.

The store staff were so impressed with Sandy Osborne's achievement—"the most well-attended local author launch in my 25 years as a bookseller," said the senior member of staff—that they hosted the launch of its sequel during normal store hours, and continued to stock both books long term.

Scottish author Wendy Jones made a similar impact with the launch event for her first novel in the Dundee branch of Waterstones:

Since the launch, Killer's Countdown *has continued to sell well. It has good product placement and has been displayed in the store window. It is always displayed cover out, rather than spine out, and it is on several tables throughout the store. I cannot thank Waterstones' Dundee branch enough for the way in which they have promoted it.*

However, the story does not stop there. The book is also stocked in several other Waterstones stores in Scotland. Following the success of my partnership with Waterstones, I approached other bookstores. CLC Bookstore in Dundee is also stocking my book. In partnership with them, we put on a Focus on Fiction week with my book as the main focus. Several weeks later, it is still in the window of the store. The Emporium, an independent bookstore in Cromarty, is also stocking it.

— WENDY JONES

Post-launch Events

Launching a new book is one good excuse for an in-store event, but there are many more. Forward-thinking bookstores whose business model identifies them as a cultural center of the community are always looking for authors to stage in-store events. It's much easier for them to involve local authors, regardless of how they are published (and possibly cheaper, if otherwise they might be expected to pay travel expenses for the guest authors).

The British chain Foyles did not discriminate between self-published and trade-published authors for its new Local Author events, and all four of the authors at its inaugural event in Bristol (my nearest branch) were self-published. I was glad to be one of them.

Some stores are even aiming at an event every night—an ambitious plan that will take some feeding. So don't be shy. Any bookstore tasked with filling its events schedule should be glad to hear from you, provided you approach them with a well-considered plan appropriate to their clientele.

Bookstores often like to tie in with national and international events:

- Olympic Games and other sporting championships
- anniversaries or centenaries that are likely to be in the public eye
- national bookseller-driven campaigns, e.g. in the US, the annual Independent Bookstore Day; in Australia, National Bookstore Day; in Canada, Authors for Indies Day; and in the UK, Independent Booksellers' Week and the Books Are My Bag campaign
- national publisher-driven campaigns, e.g. World Book Day and World Book Night.

For all of these events, bookstores will welcome suggestions. They may be planning special events and activities that are likely to increase the demand for authors in-store. While this doesn't necessarily mean they'll be more likely to stock your book at other times, it's worth investigating early to see whether there are ways that you can become involved in any events that are a good fit for your books and genre.

If you are also able to engineer an interesting event, either on your own or with one or more other authors, you may be able to persuade a bookstore to host it, especially if you promise to bring your own audience, i.e. book-buying customers.

In an interesting piece of lateral thinking, alternative history thriller writer Alison Morton joined forces with trade-published steampunk author Liesel Schwarz, to build the audiences for both of their books via joint in-store events:

Although we both write alternative worlds, Liesel with steampunk, me with alternative history, we obviously share a sense of the offbeat.

Liesel and I met through the Romantic Novelists' Association. Our books have boy-meets-girl emotional relationships, which is the crux of the matter for the RNA. As we write in speculative settings, world-building is at the forefront of our writing craft. It goes beyond setting, as we have to create a whole new world, although the characters in our books remain very human. You can imagine the discussions we have!

Although Liesel has been hailed as the new high-priestess of steampunk by The Independent *newspaper, and I've had a fair bit of success in historical and adventure fiction, neither of us is a household name, so we decided to band together to do some author talks.*

We knew were a good match for a joint event: similar enough subject areas, both outgoing communicators with successful books. Of course, having the mighty Random House PR officer helped in terms of clout; we were in The Independent's *"i" newspaper's diary under "cultural events not to be missed"! It was also a great opportunity to draw attention to my newly launched novel* Aurelia, *the fourth in my Roma Nova series.*

— ALISON MORTON

Keep a lookout for other authors' events in your area that might inspire you to formulate your own ideas. Go along to them, see what works well and what not so well, and learn from their experience. You'll also gain from attending other authors' in-store events, which offer great networking opportunities that might help your book promotion program in other ways.

In-store events will usually include at least one reading by an author, so make sure you hone your skills on reading your books aloud. ALLi news editor and Author Member Dan Holloway, an award-winning performance poet and author, explains why getting the reading, the timing, and the delivery right are so important:

I get up in front of people and say my words a lot. Both poetry and prose. I also run a lot of events. The combination gives a fascinating insight into what makes a reading work well.

The really interesting thing is that, from both sides, three minutes works incredibly well if you are putting together a series of readings.

For an organizer, with a tight schedule you have very carefully crafted so as to do right by audience, venue, and every author with their individual needs, you need people to stick to the time you have given them. Not doing so is, quite simply, rude. And three minutes of reading means five minutes per person, once you've introduced them, people have applauded, and everyone's done the shimmy to the front and back again. (When you see a time that says you're reading at 7.45 and the next person's on at 7.50, and the organizer has said you have three minutes, they really mean three minutes and these changeover rituals are why.) And five minutes is an easy time to work with.

For both of you, though, there's another reason three minutes works. And that reason is the most important thing about the whole event. Your audience. What do you both want for your audience? You want them to go away and tell everyone about these amazing writers they heard. And to just have to find the books of the ones they really loved—the books they didn't walk out with under their arm.

Which brings me to another incidental point about multi-author events and three minutes. The thing with such wonderful diverse events is that everyone will love something. And no one will love everything. And that's how it should be. And everyone's prepared to sit through three minutes of something they're not into to wait for the stuff they might really love. 27 minutes—not so much. People might leave. Because of you. That's the audience you've annoyed, and for that reason the organizer, too. And also those fellow authors who never got heard by people who might have loved them.

Anyway, back to the real reason for three minutes.

Three minutes is the standard length allowed for readings at a poetry slam, because it maximizes the author's ability to demonstrate their skills without pushing the reader's attention span to breaking. And this holds for prose as much as it does for poetry.

A great reading isn't three minutes plus "this is how I came to write the book, this is what happened previously and what is facing my character now"; it's three minutes including that. A self-contained piece needs little or no introduction.

So the perfect set? By all means give us your elevator pitch, a really witty or catchy intro, say 15–20 seconds, and allow the audience five seconds to laugh, squirm, applaud uproariously. Then read for two and a half minutes, thank everyone, and wave your book as you leave in triumph.

— DAN HOLLOWAY

Selling Print Rights to a Third Party

In an even greater piece of lateral thinking, there is another way to sell your books through bookstores, without the expense or effort of any of the activities outlined in this and the previous two chapters, and that is to sell your paperback rights to a third party, retaining only the ebook rights (which have a greater margin and lower investment required).

This position has worked very well for the likes of Hugh Howey, who, when offered a deal for his ebook and print rights, preferred to retain ebook rights, on the basis that there was nothing a publisher could do that he couldn't do himself, while trading off control of print to publishers who could offer greater presence through bookstores via their established channels than he could engineer for himself. This option is likely to be especially suitable for those who haven't yet ventured into print at all, or for those who are prepared to relinquish control in return for possibly greater sales and for not having to do any of the work of dealing with stores. It is also the way in which to get your book translated and into bookstores in other countries.

Orna Ross, ALLi director and co-author of the book *How Authors Sell Publishing Rights*, explains the choices and challenges inherent in this option, if you want to seek it out.

Traditionally—before the dawn of the ebook—the right to produce a book in a new print edition was referred to in a contract as reprint rights. Reprints come in a variety of sizes and shapes. They might include deluxe editions, large-print editions, illustrated editions, hardcover, and other special-format versions of a book. Most commonly, however, the term reprint rights refers to paperback reprint rights.

Authors and publishers choose whether a book will be published first in ebook, hardcover, or paperback. For some books, especially genre books (romance, Western, science fiction, and mystery), the first and primary format is paperback. For author–publishers, the primary format tends to be ebook and in-print, via print-on-demand. But many books are also initially distributed in a hardcover edition.

Traditionally, paperbacks were always treated as reprints of hardcover books in this way; now, trade publishers tend to purchase paperback and hardcover rights at the same time, removing paperback from the category of subsidiary right "reprints."

What is happening now is that paperback houses generally offer royalties of less than 10% gross and may also try to get you to part with ebook royalties at just 15–25% of net receipts, a poor deal for indie authors used to selling direct to readers at up to 70% commission split.

ALLi would argue that, when paperback rights are licensed by an author to another publisher, the paperback rights become a subsidiary right, with the usual subsidiary split: 50/50 publisher/author.

How this will go will depend on how much they want your book. And it's worth saying that no publisher will be interested in print rights (or translation or any other rights) unless you have proven your ability to sell a lot of books in ebook format.

Your pitch will vary depending on what rights you're looking to sell and whether you are pitching by email or in person. Either way, once you've done your market research and have your content in place (book description, review materials, etc., as well as the book itself), a good pitch is all about presentation.

Whether you're pitching to agents or publishers, think about their needs and don't be afraid to propose suggestions that might help them. As an author–publisher, you have to convince the buyer of the quality of the writing, your dedication as a writer, and your ability to reach readers.

Make your pitch easy to navigate, so people can absorb information quickly. In the words of Joseph Pulitzer, "Put it before them briefly so they will read it, clearly so they will appreciate it, picturesquely so they will remember it and, above all, accurately so they will be guided by its light."

Here are some useful tips to bear in mind when pitching:

- **Research:** Thoroughly research the agency or publisher, getting into their skin and thinking about ways your book enhances their offering, extends the discoverability of their other books, and helps them meet their goals.
- **Professional:** Whether pitching to an agent who can help you sell your rights, or directly to a publisher, your presentation should be simple, clean, and professional, i.e. in the proper file format with the appropriate tone and voice. Copy should be clean and demonstrate sufficient knowledge and skill. Avoid gimmicks like crazy fonts or pictures; these only detract from your pitch.
- **Clarity:** Make it clear what is available to read now and what you hope the agent or publisher will achieve for you. Say why you write and who you identify as your audience. If you have been trade-published or have had an agent before, give details.
- **Honest dealing:** No hiding, subterfuge, or trying to put one over on anyone. If this is a multiple submission, say so.
- **Passion:** Be passionate about your work. Don't boast or drone on and on, but don't be afraid to show enthusiasm and tout your success. Practice a way of doing this without overselling or sounding immodest.
- **Success:** List your achievements, presenting your ideas and your work clearly, simply, and without hyperbole. If you have stats or analytics, prizes or sales points, here is the place to share them. Say what you have already published,

what you have already written, and what you see as long-term and achievable goals. Give examples of your success throughout the entire pitch.

- **Openness:** Listen to what the agent or publisher is saying and ask follow-up questions. See what you can learn. Show true and sincere passion while being open to feedback.
- **Language:** Think about the language you use to describe your books and your ambitions. One agent we know recommends saying "our" and "we" early on in the pitch, already subtly including yourself in the agent or publisher's team.
- **Questions:** Anticipate likely questions and prepare your answers. Make a list of questions to ask, and do ask them.
- **Strengths:** Highlight your strengths and where you add value. If you've got specialist skills that are rare to find, or something that no one else can offer (and most of us have), tell the agent or publisher. So many writers are hopeless at this. Practice and get better.
- **Be yourself, warts and all:** Don't be afraid to admit to gaps or weaknesses. Relax and smile, be friendly, and don't be afraid to crack the odd joke. Keep things light and be genuinely interested in the people you're pitching to. People always want to work with people they like; people like people who like them.

It bears mentioning that you need to know when the rules can be bent. Sometimes the conventional method of doing things is less effective than getting creative. If your pitch still holds true to Pulitzer's advice, and these general guidelines, it doesn't need to lockstep in line with all the "rules." There are no rules; there is only what works.

Don't be quirky or different just for the sake of it, however. If you choose to color outside the lines, it needs to be consistent with and illustrative of your pitch.

For a detailed consideration of rights issues, read ALLi's

guidebook *How Authors Sell Publishing Rights* by Orna Ross and Helen Sedwick.

Ways of Selling Print Books Online

And finally, a reminder that bookstores are not the only places to sell print books. Although the majority of books sold online are ebooks, online retailers offer an opportunity to make significant sales in print too.

Marketing programs designed to promote ebooks, such as Amazon Marketing Services for Kindle books, may have a knock-on effect on the print sales of an ebook, because the ad is also seen by readers who only buy print.

At ALLi we are also seeing a growing number of authors who are selling print books directly from their own websites.

HOW I DO IT: ALLI MEMBERS' BOOKSTORE EXPERIENCES

As evidence of how, with the right product, approach, and attitude, indie authors can sell self-published books through bookstores, here are some encouraging case studies from ALLi members around the world.

Prue Batten, Australia

When I first indie published in 2008 (Book One of *The Chronicles of Eirie*—a historical fantasy), my local Dymocks store was absolutely fabulous. They ordered my books from Ingram because I was a local writer, stocked them on the front pedestal of the store, and they subsequently told me they sold more of that title than any other new-release author they had profiled.

When I became indie, I always said my books had to survive on their own merits—no consignment: independent orders from bookstores and readers only. It worked!

Dymocks in Tasmania is a lateral-thinking store with a tremendous attitude toward reader and writer alike, and I love them.

Di Castle, England

I have always used my local bookstore, New and Secondhand Books, Station Road, Swanage, and before my book came out I visited more often and cultivated a good relationship with the owner, Jill Blanchard. I checked that the publisher had sent an advance information sheet, and said I would get the owner some Facebook likes and publicize it when she stocked my book. She has taken two deliveries direct from me of ten books and sold them, and is now on her second lot of five since Christmas. *Grandma's Poetry Book* has been in the window twice, first for a whole month before Christmas and then for a couple of weeks around Mother's Day. I take her my homespun fliers, which are targeted for her (no Amazon mention), and she has been putting them in bags when people buy other books. I abandoned Amazon for purchases and now order my books through her shop. I have promoted her on Facebook and Twitter and pop in regularly to check how many copies are there. She charges a favorable local author rate. I have my book in four other Dorset bookstores by taking in a sample copy or posting one for review preceded by a phone call. Altogether I have been delighted with how receptive these independent bookstores have been.

Larry Garner, US

I have two books published independently and, although I had no trouble whatsoever displaying my books in independent, local bookstores in town, I had no luck with the big boys on the high street. Of course, my main target was the local airport bookstore, but getting in there seemed impossible. Twice I approached the owner of the bookstore. Twice I was politely told there wasn't sufficient shelf space. But I did have better luck with the manager. I approached her and said I would split the sales with her 50/50 while she was on duty. She agreed.

We have a rather large fly-in fly-out population (FIFO, mainly mining) in our location and, as both of my books are related to the mining industry, I targeted the flights most of the FIFOs took. I arrived a couple of hours before the flight and set up a small but very prominent stand in a corner of the shop, advertised the books as the "amusing tales of a FIFO miner," but pricing it was the winner: most books in the shop were priced between $24 and $29. I priced my books at $12.50. I sold out! I sold over a hundred books in two hours. Of course, the manager was the real winner; she took home over $600 for doing absolutely nothing. But don't think I wasn't happy.

Helena Halme, Finnish Author Based in London

I couldn't be an author without the constant support of an active independent shop, such as West End Lane Books. Just entering through the door, when that indescribable smell of (good) books hits you, you know you're among friends.

West End Lane Books is a small indie shop nestling in the arty northwest London area of West Hampstead. The shop stocks a varied and interesting selection of books, and as well as hosting events with authors, they run two book clubs. One is aptly named West End Crooks, just for crime fiction, and the other is a more traditional book club. All clubbers get a 15% discount on the month's read. The @WELBooks Twitter feed is active and often hilarious.

West End Lane Books have supported my writing from the very beginning, when I decided to go indie and lived locally. They've stocked my first published novel, *The Englishman*, and also *Coffee and Vodka*, which made it into their "Staff Favorites" and keeps selling out. They also always have one or two signed copies of my books, which they hand-sell.

Katherine Hayton, New Zealand

I'm giving a shout-out to a bookstore that's recently opened in Upper Hutt, New Zealand. Named Writers Plot Readers Read (after a well-established writing group in the area named Writer's Plot), the bookstore is operating as a nonprofit determined to bring indie and self-published New Zealand writers into a bricks-and-mortar bookstore, often for the first time.

They have a few minimum checks to ensure the writing is up to their quality standards, but otherwise every NZ indie author is welcome to stock there.

They feature a rotating writer-in-residence program, which means book buyers can get to meet and talk with some of the authors that they're purchasing, and they also run a lot of writer's workshops to help writers develop their craft. A writing desk is also able to be hired out in-store for a small fee if writers need somewhere to get away from their raucous daily life.

How's that for the perfect writing space, in the middle of a bookstore? Mmmmm. The smell of new books!

Karen Inglis, England

I'm stocked by and have been supporting my local bookstores over the past few years, both the small independents and Waterstones in southwest London. They really do appreciate the support we can bring through events and also helping point customers their way via social media and through fliers, etc. if holding events with them. It had been on my to-do list for months to add a link to the "Find your local bookstore" sites in the UK and the US to my author site and my blog, and I finally got around to doing that. I have always offered links to the bookstores local to me, but offering links to the search pages of IndieBound is another way we can support our local and not-so-local bricks-and-mortar stores.

Maggie Lynch Jamieson, US

I have been blessed to work with over twenty-five bookstores in the Pacific Northwest (US) to place my books. It began as a consignment and mutual marketing partnership. Most bookstores in my area take on indie authors first on consignment. I give them between two and five books on a 40% discount. Depending on the store, they stock those books for two to six months. If they have not sold after the designated period, I have to pick them up.

Fortunately, in all the bookstores my five books usually sell out within one month. This means that now those bookstores buy my books in advance, instead of me having to consign them, because I have a track record of selling. I have found that if I do things for them (plan signing events with me and other authors in similar genres), market to my network along with their marketing efforts, and occasionally write a guest post for their newsletters, it garners me recognition with their clients, and the booksellers are happy to hand-sell my books.

Though I have twenty-five wonderful stores, there are two that are standouts, not only for me, but which actively seek indie authors and their books. Jan's Paperbacks, owned by Debbie Burke, in Aloha, Oregon, and Another Read Through, owned by Elisa Saphir, in Portland, Oregon.

Chris Longmuir, Scotland

I approached my local branch of the UK bookstore chain Waterstones, in Dundee, but it was a different manager to now because this was way back in 2013. I traveled to Dundee with two copies of each of my books, and muttering under my breath that the worst that could happen would be a refusal. Quaking in my shoes, I delivered my spiel to the manager, showed him the books, and was amazed when he ordered twenty copies of each book. Needless to say I delivered them the next day.

Later that same year, Waterstone's launched my new book in the Dundee Crime Series, *Missing Believed Dead*, with an order of sixty copies of the book. The launch was a great success, and Waterstones ran out of chairs for those attending, so it was standing room only at the back. They continue to give me regular orders, and also launched my historical crime mystery, *The Death Game*, in 2014.

Apart from Waterstones, my books are stocked by my local book shop, Hoggs of Montrose, and I receive regular orders from Gardners and Bertrams, the major distributors of books in the UK.

Yvonne Payne, Crete

Kritsotopoula, Girl of Kritsa has its basis in a true story set in our home village of Kritsa on the Greek island of Crete. In the nearby holiday resort of Elounda, the wonderful Eklektos Bookstore is popular with locals and holidaymakers alike. I decided that, if the owner of Eklektos, Lynne McDonald, read my draft novel and agreed to stock it as a paperback, I would go ahead with publication. Not only did Lynne agree to stock the book but she also acts as my distributor to get the books into Crete. We now take every opportunity to give each other support, knowing that what is good for one of us is good for the other.

Mohanalakshmi Rajakumar, Qatar

When I first entered self-publishing I was learning about ebooks. I had eight manuscripts that had been politely declined by well-meaning agents in a ten-year period. Feeling like the literary version of a spinster, ebooks catapulted me into using the title of writer officially with friends and family. Two years later, I was ready to launch a paperback. At the time, I didn't know the first thing about scheduling book events. I asked friends for recommendations of cafés that held events.

Christmas of 2012 we left our son with family to rush across town, wondering if anyone would even show up. They did. About twelve people, most of them friends who wanted to catch up.

"You don't know me, but I follow your blog," a bearded, spectacled man said, striding in with his daughter. An electric current ran through the rest of us. This is real, my husband's look said. Hope you have something good to say.

That same year, a few weeks later, we were staring at a "Closed" sign in Georgia, the supposed second stop of the book tour. The café had forgotten the New Year's Day event they had agreed to. We went to the movies instead.

I tried again six months later, as my new plan was to release all the ebooks as paperbacks, two a year. I wised up to independent bookstores and libraries, the living rooms of friends, and more or less anyone who wanted to talk to me about one of my books.

Some of them were great fun, like reunions, hugging old friends I hadn't seen in years, who kindly bought multiple copies of each title. Some of them were embarrassing, like the phone call I had to make while sitting alone at a signing table. "That's okay," I told the manager, who apologized for the fact no one said a word to me during my hour and a half vigil. (Except for the guy who chatted to me for ten minutes, ending with "I don't read books. Bye.") I didn't want to be a prima donna, since he had warned me volubly about low attendance before agreeing to host me. I drove away as quickly as I could.

In April, visiting Tampa for a conference, I began emailing bookstores, asking if anyone wanted to host me and my two paperbacks, the memory of that solitary event hovering in the shadows. "We don't do book events," came one gruff reply.

"Hi, this is Mohana. I sent you an email about doing a book event," I said to the person on the other end at the Old Tampa Book Company. I busied myself with my Twitter timeline to delay the sting of another brush-off.

"Yes, sorry, I've been so busy, but we would love to host you."

"You would?" I sat up straighter.

The conference I attended that month in Tampa had me scratching my head. "What am I doing here?" I thought, suppressing yawns at heavily academic presentations. That night I assembled myself for the event. And I was amazed by the wonderful people who showed up— strangers!—who hung on the edge of their seats and bought multiple copies of both my books. They had come in because of the strength of the shop's mailing list. "We did better sales on your night than we have all week," the shop owner said to me with a huge smile.

"Yes, thanks for being persistent," laughed the events person at a feminist bookstore in Atlanta. "We would love to have you."

Again in New York, strangers came into the volunteer-run shop, Bluestockings, to sit, listen, and ask questions about my work. They waited for me to sign copies for their friends and families.

In 2015 I did a five-stop book tour, in independent bookstores from New York to Atlanta. None of this would have happened without persistence and humility. (Not to mention writing new books.) If you have a story to tell, keep telling it. Keep asking—someone will definitely say yes.

Lorna Sixsmith, Ireland

I love how owners of independent bookstores know about books and will recommend good ones to readers. I was invited to a readers' event in a bookstore last December, and I was so excited when I went in and saw she had cupcakes with little book covers on each one. I was the least well-known author there. I was delighted to have my book cupcakes beside Martine Madden's, Liz Nugent's, and Donal Ryan's!

Debbie Young, England

Living 100 miles from my native London, I'd never have dreamed of trying to hold a London launch for *Best Murder in Show*, the first novel in my new Sophie Sayers Village Mysteries series, as I have no established contacts with any bookstores there. Then I came across an organization called Novel London, which runs a series of monthly reading events in various central London branches of Waterstones. Novel London's founder, Safeena Chaudhry, has a good relationship with the retail chain, and so by working in tandem with her, I was able to share a stage for a joint event with fellow ALLi crime writer JJ Marsh, who was launching her latest Beatrice Stubbs thriller, *Bad Apples*, compered by ALLi author Rohan Quine. The store ordered twenty copies of my novel from IngramSpark, we had a packed house with standing room only, and we had our names and books promoted in-store and on the Waterstones website before the event, as well as on Novel London's. I also got a professional-standard video for my own website as part of the deal. ALLi teamwork at its finest!

WHY EVERY AUTHOR NEEDS BOOKSTORES

Even if the preceding chapters have not convinced you to try to get your self-published books into bookstores, having persuaded you that your book will do better sold exclusively online or elsewhere, please do not turn your back on bookstores, assuming they will play no part in your success as an indie author. I would like to make the case for supporting bookstores in other ways, for the long-term good of your career. Here's why.

No Author is an Island

If bookstores continue to disappear from our shopping locations, individual authors and the whole breed of authors will be diminished. Because doesn't it help us all if bookstores continue to present to shoppers of all ages the notion that Buying Books Is A Good Thing? That instead of spending their disposable income on clothes or shoes or electronics or toiletries, they'd be better to invest in something fabulous to read? That rather than buy birthday and Christmas presents from random shops that they're unsure the recipients would like, a great book or a book token would be a better solution?

Bookstores, like libraries and schoolteachers, are ambassadors for the joy of reading—and all authors need readers. Unless these players keep shouting the message that reading is cool and fun, and an affordable source of joy and inspiration for all ages, our society risks forgetting the power of the written word. We'll all be too busy filling our leisure hours with television-on-demand, listen-again radio, and the frenzy that is social media.

Bookstores Help ebooks

Even if we don't publish print books, and stick to ebook only, we should still support physical bookstores, even though by driving shoppers into their stores, we're showing them the range of competition to our own books. But hey, they'll be exposed to an awful lot more of the competition if they buy our books online.

Actually, by supporting our local bookstores, or indeed any other bookstores, such as charity (thrift) stores or the dreaded remainder booksellers, where trade-published books go on reprieve from being pulped, we come away inspired and motivated, as if our creative batteries have had a quick recharge. Visiting bookstores also helps us strengthen our relationship with the stockists who do carry our books.

So really, what's not to love about bricks-and-mortar bookstores? Next time you're on the high street, make sure you visit yours.

Here are twenty easy actions within your power to help bookstores survive, multiply, and thrive. Most of them will cost you little or nothing to carry out. None of them ranks as rocket science, but they're every bit as practical. And every time you do one, you'll be paying it forward.

As well as helping to build a better relationship between authors and booksellers everywhere, you'll be bonding better with your own local store, and so making it more likely that if they're not yet stocking your books, maybe they will some day.

Ways to Help Bookstores

1. Buy books! If you plan to buy a book, and have a bricks-and-mortar store near you, buy it there. If the book you want is not in stock, the store can usually get it for you just as fast as any online ordering service. It may not be cheaper, but you'll be able to buy it with a clear conscience!
2. Give books—as gifts (so easy to wrap and post at Christmas and birthdays).
3. Buy book tokens or bookstore vouchers—only able to be spent in dedicated bookstores and a great way to encourage children and young people to acquire the benefits of a reading habit. Yes, they might rather have an iTunes token, but book tokens have gone zonking up in the cool stakes with trendy plastic credit-card style designs. Didn't you love to receive book tokens when you were a kid? Pay that joy forward to the next generation, and you'll be helping a bookstore at the same time.
4. If your books are stocked in a particular shop, add it as a list of stockists on your author website. To ensure they continue to be stocked, you need to drive a pull-through of demand: getting the books stocked is just the first part of the process. Don't just list the usual Amazon affiliate links or whatever, which earn you peanuts in any case, and are more effective in fueling Amazon's empire than your bank account. (It will also score you a point with any local bookstore looking you up on Amazon—much better than if, when they visit your website, they find you're driving all your readers away from the high street to online retailers, like some evil Pied Piper of the book trade.)
5. Remind people to support their local bookstore, shop local, or however you prefer to word it. If their local bookstore (which in most cases won't be the same as yours) doesn't already stock your book, suggest they ask the proprietor to

order your book for them. Your readers will be happy to receive that message, whether or not they choose to follow it. And if enough people start clamoring for your book in any particular shop, it's likely the proprietor will start keeping it in stock for as long as the demand continues.

6. Resolve to visit your nearest bookstore whenever you are on the high street or at the mall. Become a regular face there, befriend the staff, and before you know it, you'll find an opportunity to tell them about your book, even if you didn't have any intention of selling it there. Don't be shy of telling them about your book (or worse still, go in with a sense of entitlement)—most booksellers will consider authors premium-value customers, whether or not they stock your book, because they will perceive you as moving in circles where reading is king and having your own tribe of avid readers, to whom you're likely to recommend other books as well as your own.

7. Support other authors' events there. Whether or not you're interested in the author or their book, it's another way to become a familiar face and known supporter of the store. You'll also pick up tips on how to run an author event (or not!) and might even gain a new author friend to add to your own network.

8. Keep track of the kind of events they hold there, which they'll have carefully chosen to suit their clientele, and see if you can dream up one of your own in a similar mold, either on your own or with indie author friends. Then go all out to bring an audience with you that buys books at the event, whether yours or others. Stage a successful event and you may even get asked back for more—because each time they see you in future, they'll have dollar/euro/pound signs in their eyes, seeing you as an asset to their business.

9. If you're staging local events elsewhere, show your support for the bookstore by inviting them—not to run a shop for you, but as a guest. Whether or not they wish to come, ask

for a stack of their promotional fliers or bookmarks to give
to your audience to promote their bookstore.

10. If your local bookstore runs a festival, as many do, offer
your services as a volunteer. Most festivals, small or large,
like the Olympics, rely on an army of volunteers to be
financially viable. (*Opening Up To Indie Authors* published by
ALLi provides a useful reality check on the economics of
festivals.) Volunteers tend to be either avid readers or
aspiring authors, as I discovered when I was buttonholed by
a small crowd of volunteers after the audience had left a talk
for authors that I gave at Cambridge Lit Fest last year. A
great opportunity not only to score points with your
bookstore but to network with potential readers and make
new like-minded friends. Do it enough and the bookstore
will start to see you as one of their ambassadors, which will
make them more likely to be ambassadors for your
book too.

11. If there are national bookish events going on that your local
store is likely to engage in, you should also embrace them. If
you're a children's or YA (young adult) author, World Book
Day provides a great opportunity to support your local
bookstore by going in to be a resident author for the day,
helping run activities for visiting children. If you're a World
Book Night book giver, you can designate your local
bookstore as your pick-up point—an easy way to declare
yourself as a passionate advocate of books and reading,
rather than an egotistical author thinking only of your own
book's sales.

12. If they hold a book group, or book groups meet in their
store, either offer to be a guest speaker to the book group,
or join it as a reader—again, a great networking
opportunity that will lead to other advantages.

13. There are a lot of things you can do to support the
bookstore without even leaving your desk, such as like their
Facebook page, comment on their posts, share their posts;

follow them on Twitter, RT key posts, #FF them for Follow Fridays. Subscribe to their online newsletter. (Being a bookseller can feel like a thankless task sometimes, and strategic social media sharing can make their day—and probably earn some shares of your posts by return.)

14. If you blog, and host guests, consider doing an interview with your local bookstore proprietor or staff. If you're a book blogger, consider also giving a shout-out to high street bookstores that you love, adding to them as you find more on your travels and on holiday.

15. If they have an in-store loyalty card, sign up for one. You'll earn points or other benefits, and you'll also be helping them build greater knowledge of their local customers, Amazon style.

16. Ask if you could take a photo of the store to go on your website. There's bound to be somewhere you can use it as an illustration, even if they don't stock your book. Then, when you use it, send them a link, which they may even share, or which might drive them to consider stocking your book in future.

17. Ask whether they could spare a supply of their branded bookmarks to be included in every copy of your book that you hand-sell. You're effectively offering them free advertising space in front of a book buyer.

18. Use their facilities—by which I don't mean the loo! But if they have a coffee shop, and you plan to meet friends for coffee, or you want to eat out while you're shopping, use their coffee shop. I've never visited a bookish coffee shop I didn't like. I even refer to the Bristol Foyles' coffee shop as my Bristol office, and I'm only half joking. It's my city-center place of choice for meetings with other authors, whether on a friendly basis or as one of my book promotion consultancy slots, and the chances of us both leaving the shop without buying a book as well as a coffee are pretty slim. In fact, I consider buying a book notional rent for my

Bristol office—and if I really can't think of a book I want, I can always buy a greetings card or a notebook.

19. Show simple kindness and good manners: when buying a book, smile, chat (unless they're hugely busy), say something nice, and thank them for their help. My local bookstore proprietor makes no secret of the fact that he always welcomes gifts of coffee from the nearby bakery.

20. Treat staff like the professionals that you both are. If you're seeking a book for a particular purpose, ask for and respect their advice. Their expertise never fails to amaze me, especially when compared with the mechanical and often entertaining/horrifying recommendations from online searches, where the results are provided by algorithms rather than human beings, at least at the storefront level.

Although we may be grateful to online retailers and distribution platforms for empowering the modern author, there is room in the lives and businesses of authorpreneurs for retailers of all kinds. We lose any of these parties at our peril.

So let's work together to keep bookstores on the high street as a universal temple to the author's trade, as embassies of reading, for the greater good of booksellers, writers, and readers all over the world.

The takeaway message is very simple: ask not what bookstores can do for you—but what you can do for bookstores.

GOING FORWARD TOGETHER

At ALLi, we hope that this book, offered as part of our educational program, will unite and empower indie authors and bookstores alike to work long term for mutual benefit, together riding whatever other changes may arise in this fast-evolving business.

This book is just part of ALLi's continuing program to harmonize and synchronize the different worlds of author and bookseller. We will also:

- share the latest headlines regarding the book trade in the Author Advice Centre's (AAC) weekly news roundup
- run informative posts in the Book Marketing section of the AAC blog
- publish case studies of authors and bookstores working effectively together to inspire others to follow suit
- include events celebrating bookstores in our online calendar of global events of interest to authors
- encourage authors to support bookstores however they can, as listed in the chapter "Why Every Author Needs Bookstores"

- celebrate and highlight innovations that continue to make physical bookstores such special places, offering so much that is not available in the online retail environment
- use our #Authors4Bookstores hashtag wherever possible to fly the flag for this philosophy.

At the same time, we have the greatest respect for authors who have decided not to pursue bookstores as a retail outlet. After all, as indie authors, that is their prerogative, and it is the combination of our independence with our mutual support that makes the world of self-publishing such an exciting and rewarding arena for us all.

If you're inspired by this book to take steps into selling via bookstores, do let us how you get on by commenting on the ALLi blog or emailing us through our contact form.

And if you'd like to continue the learning, we'd love to have you as an ALLi member. Even if you haven't published yet, you are welcome as an associate member. More information at allianceindependentauthors.org.

BOOKS THAT FEATURE BOOKSTORES

84 Charing Cross Road—Helene Hanff
The Bookseller of Kabul—Åsne Seierstad
Shadow of the Wind—Carlos Ruiz Zafon
The Bookshop Book—Jen Campbell
Books, Baguettes and Bedbugs—Jeremy Mercer
Weird Things Customers Say in Bookshops and (inevitably, because there must be an endless supply of material) *More Weird Things Customers Say in Bookshops*—Jen Campbell
The Yellow-Lighted Bookstore: A Memoir, A History—Lewis Buzbee
The Bookstore—Penelope Fitzgerald
You—Caroline Kepnes

AUTHORS WHO HAVE BEEN BOOKSELLERS

MC Beaton
Jen Campbell
Penelope Fitzgerald
Suzie Grogan
Helena Halme
Susan Hill
Hugh Howey
Rachel Joyce
David Nicholls
Louise Walters

GLOSSARY

A

abook
Abbreviation of audiobook. *Compare:* pbook and ebook.

acknowledgments
Recognition or honor given to people who have influenced a book or who have made a difference in the life of the author.

ACOS (average cost of sale)
Accumulated total of all costs used to create a product or service, including overheads, fixed and variable costs.

acquisitions board
A group of people who work for a publisher to make decisions about what books to accept for publication.

ACX (Audiobook Creation Exchange)
An Amazon-owned marketplace that matches authors with professional narrators and producers for the creation of audiobooks (abooks).

advance
An upfront payment made by a publisher, as an advance on expected

royalties, in exchange for the rights to publish and sell your book(s) and associated rights.

advance information sheet (AIS)
A short document providing basic book details and information about a book's availability and ordering methods. *Also:* sell sheet.

advance print run
Printing of a book completed before the book's official release date, usually for publicity purposes.

advance review copy (ARC)
A draft of a book sent to beta readers or reviewers prior to publication. *Also:* advance review/reader copy. *Compare:* proof.

aggregator
A service provider that publishes and distributes books to a variety of distributors and retailers. *Compare:* distributor.

algorithm
A process or set of rules used in a calculation; book retailers like Amazon use algorithms to calculate a book's sales ranking.

Amazon Author Central
A free resource that allows you to publish an Author Profile and feature books on Amazon.

Amazon Marketing Services (AMS)
An Amazon program that allows sellers to bid on advertisements displayed alongside search results, product listings, and customer review pages.

Amazon Prime
A subscription service for Amazon customers that offers discounted shipping, access to free entertainment, and other benefits.

Amazon Standard Identification Number (ASIN)
A unique, ten-character identifier for an Amazon product.

appendix
Part of a book that follows a chapter or that comes after all the chapters, with supplemental matter, such as tables or source material.

AskALLi
Alliance of Independent Authors campaign that pledges to answer any self-publishing question that any individual or organization may have.

assisted (self-)publisher
A company that provides book production, distribution, marketing, and other services to self-publishers.

Audible
An Amazon-owned company; the largest audiobook producer and retailer in the US.

audiobook
A recording of a book or magazine being read aloud.

author bio
A brief biography that may include a summary of books written, interests, and achievements.

author brand
A representation of your identity and image that helps your readers connect with you and your books.

author cooperative/collective
A group of authors who work together to leverage the skills of the group in order to advance members' publishing efforts.

author platform
The ability to sell books because of who you are or can reach.

authorpreneur
An author who successfully runs a publishing business.

author–publisher
A professional self-publisher writing for profit.

Authors4Bookstores
Alliance of Independent Authors campaign connecting writers and booksellers, for mutual benefit.

Author Solutions, Inc. (ASI)
A notorious vanity press operating under a variety of imprints.

B

Babelcube
Company that connects authors with translators and internationally distributes translated books.

back matter

The sections of a book following the last chapter. *Also* end matter. *Compare:* front matter.

bar code

An image that encodes information into a series of vertical lines; a book's ISBN encoded in this format.

Bertrams

The second-largest book wholesaler in the UK.

bestseller rank

See: sales rank.

beta reader

A person who provides early feedback or a critique of a book prior to publication.

big data

An enormous supply of data, and often the analysis of such data.

Big Five

The five largest, New York-based traditional publishers: Hachette, HarperCollins, Macmillan, Penguin Random House, and Simon & Schuster. Formerly the "Big Six," until the merger of Penguin and Random House in 2013.

BISAC

An acronym for Book Industry Standards and Communications.

BISAC codes

The BISAC subject headings list; a standard used to categorize books based on topical content.

bitcoin

The most popular cryptocurrency, generally deemed the first of its kind. The open source software comes with an elusive and mysterious history. Satoshi Nakamoto is the name used by the unknown person(s) who designed the bitcoin, but no one is really sure who made it.

bleed

To extend an element that is printed right up to the page edge, such as an image or background tint, beyond the trim size to allow for variations in trimming.

blockchain

As part of the implementation of Bitcoin, the first blockchain database was devised to record the cryptocurrency transactions. Blockchain technology operates as a public, verified digital ledger that records transactions as a chain (string) of data, stored on a decentralized network. Information, once entered, can't be altered. Blockchain also has several non-cryptocurrency applications, including smart contracts and the recording of other digital assets.

blog

A regularly updated section on your website; a useful way to help you establish your subject matter expertise and connect with your readers.

blog hop

A list of web links that appears on multiple blogs, allowing readers to hop from one blog to the next in the series. *Also:* link-up.

blog tour

A series of pre-arranged blog posts, usually scheduled during the months just before and after a book launch.

Book2Look

A widget offering samples from your book alongside social links.

BookBaby

An ebook publisher and aggregator.

book block

PDF files that comprise all book content except the cover. *See also:* interior.

book blurb

A short description of a book, often used on the back cover.

BookBub

An ebook discovery service featuring a free daily email that notifies readers of discounted ebooks.

book categories

See: BISAC.

book chainstores

Book outlets that share a brand and central management, usually with standardized business methods and practices, and spread nationwide or worldwide.

book doctoring
See: content editing.

Book Espresso machine
A machine that can print and bind any book as print-on-demand within five minutes.

book fair
An exhibition and convention for publishers, authors, and booksellers.

book review
See: review.

Booksellers Association of Great Britain and Ireland (BA)
The trade association for booksellers.

Books In Print
A catalog, usually digital, primarily for use by bookstores and libraries, listing millions of books with ISBNs; published by Bowker.

book trailer
A video advertisement for a book, much the same as a film trailer.

Bowker
A for-profit corporation that is the sole provider of and registrar for ISBNs in the US.

bricks-and-mortar (brick) bookstore
A physical store; said of a retailer, in contrast to online operations.

C

call to action (CTA)
The part of a marketing message that attempts to persuade a person to perform a desired action.

case bound
A type of binding and the industry term for a book in hardback/hardcover format.

click-through
The process of clicking on a hyperlink or online advertisement to the target destination.

click-through open rate (CTOR)
Metrics used to measure the effectiveness of your email marketing campaigns.

click-through rate (CTR)
The average number of click-throughs per hundred ad impressions, expressed as a percentage.

CMYK
A color model for print books, using cyan (C), magenta (M), yellow (Y), and black (K). *See also:* RGB, greyscale.

codex
A physical book which may be constructed of vellum, papyrus, or similar materials, as well as paper, and handwritten or printed.

collaborative consumption
An economic model based on the sharing, swapping, and renting of services. The "sharing economy" or "collaborative economy" can be seen in platforms like Airbnb or Kickstarter and is growing in fintech (financial technology), through solutions like peer-to-peer lending.

commission (1)
A percentage of book sales paid to the author. Often used interchangeably with royalties.

commission (2)
To order or authorize the production of publications, services or materials.

content editing
Editing with a focus on broad issues such as pacing, character development, veracity, relevance, and structure. *Also:* structural editing, development(al) editing, book doctoring, or manuscript appraisal.

content editor
The person who conducts a content edit.

content marketing
The creation and sharing of useful material like videos, blogs, and social media posts to generate leads for your book.

conversion
The process of putting a manuscript into a digital format suitable for

use by a publisher, such as converting a Word document into an EPUB file.

co-op advertising

Advertising whose cost is shared between or among different companies. Such advertising is especially advantageous to smaller companies with limited budgets.

copyediting

Editing with a focus on the detail, such as syntax, grammar, verb tense, word usage, punctuation, and consistency. *Also:* line editing.

copyeditor

The person who conducts a copyedit of your copy (manuscript material).

copyright

The exclusive legal right to publish, perform, or record a literary work, to profit from it, and to authorize others to do the same. *Compare:* license.

cost per click (CPC)

Internet advertising model used to direct traffic to websites, in which an advertiser pays a website owner when their advertisement is clicked. Also used to refer to the cost charged for each click through from the ad to the product. *Also:* pay per click.

cost per impression (CPI)

Also known as pay per impression. Internet advertising model, in which advertisers pay for the number of times an ad is shown on a website, regardless of whether or not it is clicked. *Also:* pay per impression.

co-venture

Undertaking whose costs and responsibilities are shared by more than one company or publisher.

cover design

Aesthetic layout on the covers of a book, usually intended to be attractive or alluring to the eye.

cover spread

The entire cover of a physical book, from the front, including the spine, to the back.

CreateSpace
An Amazon-owned publisher and distributor of self-published print books.

credit line
Line of text that assigns credit to the owner of the copyright of the material it refers to.

critique
See: content editing.

crowd-
A prefix used to denote a collaborative effort by a group.

crowdfunding
Funding a project by raising small donations from many contributors.

crowdsourcing
Gathering information, feedback, or work on a project by requesting input from a large number of contributors.

cryptocurrency
Any digital currency, operating independently of a central bank, using encryption techniques to regulate the generation, verification, and transfer of funds. Using cryptography for regulation and security allows a decentralized system, meaning no central repository or administrator oversees the processes. Instead, it uses a blockchain. There are several kinds of cryptocurrency; three of the best known to date are bitcoin, ethereum, and ripple.

customer acquisition cost (CAC)
Measuring how much money a new customer has cost you.

D

dashboard
An interface, usually web-based, that organizes and displays information on a single screen.

database
A program that allows you to organize your information in an efficient manner on one platform.

dedication
Part of the front matter that dedicates a book to a specific person,
place, or thing.

Demy Octavo
A very popular book format, which measures 216 x 138 mm.

developmental editing
See: content editing.

developmental editor
Person who deals with the overall organization of a manuscript rather
than with detailed changes such as spelling and punctuation.

digital printing
A method of mass-production printing using toners on a press
printing direct from a digital-based image. More suitable for shorter
runs and most often used for print-on-demand books. *Compare:* offset
printing.

digital wallet
Any electronic device or application that allows electronic
transactions, using cryptocurrency or government-based currencies.

discounts
There are two kinds of discounts in publishing: retail discount, when
books are offered at a reduced sale price to the reader; and publisher's
discount, offered to wholesalers, distributors, and retailers.

discoverability
The process of making something discoverable for consumers.

disintermediation
The removal of intermediaries from a supply chain or cutting out the
middleman in a transaction.

distributed ledger
A distributed ledger (also called shared ledger) is a consensus of
replicated, shared, and synchronized digital data geographically
spread across multiple sites, countries, or institutions where there is
no central administrator or centralized data storage.

distributor
A service that makes books available for purchase by bricks-and-
mortar or online retailers. *Compare:* aggregator.

DOC, DOCX
Microsoft Word file types.

domain name
A registered alias for an IP address; the most basic URL of a website, e.g. "selfpublishingadvice.org".

DPI (dots per inch)
A measure of the resolution of a graphic file, a computer monitor, or potential printing density.

Draft2Digital
A popular ebook aggregator and publishing service.

dust jacket
A detachable outer cover that protects the book, printed with the cover design. Usually for hardback/hardcover books.

E

ebook
An abbreviation of electronic (digital) book.

editorial review
A professional critic's opinion of a book published online or in a periodical. *See also:* review.

eID/electronic identity
Identity in a digital format. Often involves an identity card with embedded chip, certification, separate signatures for authentication and verification, etc. eID is legally binding and used to sign smart contracts in a number of countries.

email marketing
The promotion of products or services to list subscribers via email.

em dash and en dash
The en dash (longer than a **hyphen**) connects things that are related to each other by distance or range, as in the May–September issue of a magazine (also including June, July, and August). The em dash (longer than an en dash) is used to add an additional thought within a sentence, or to substitute for something missing. *See also:* hyphen.

encryption
The process of encoding messages. Encryption is vital to fintech, the blockchain, and anything else that needs to be secure. Data, like names and numbers, is turned into a code using algorithms (mathematical formulas). A key is required to turn that code back into useful data.

encumber
To license a right to another party, thereby creating restrictions on how that right may be used in the future.

end matter
See: back matter.

endorsement quotes
Short reviews of your book written by a well-known author, professional, or personality in your author niche.

epilogue
A section or chapter at the end of a book that comment on or draws conclusions about what has happened or been explained within the text.

EPUB
A common ebook file format.

epublishing
The publication of digital works such as ebooks.

ereader
A handheld device on which electronic versions of books, newspapers, magazines, etc. can be read.

etailer
An online retailer.

ether
The native cryptocurrency of the Ethereum platform, used to pay for computational services there.

Ethereum
A blockchain-based cryptocurrency platform that runs smart contracts, already in use by writers and artists.

Ethical Author
Alliance of Independent Authors campaign encouraging and educating authors in best practices in writing and publishing.

exclusivity
A publishing contract that binds you solely to one publisher. In self-publishing, being exclusive to one particular store or retailer.

F

Facebook ad
Advertising via Facebook that allows you to choose your target audience based on demographics, behavior, or contact information.
fintech
Financial technology that is allowing the disruption of traditional financial networks, facilitating innovation and the possibility of an author-centric financial model.
first rights
The exclusive right to publish a work for the first time.
font
A specific typeface of a certain size and style. *Compare:* typeface.
footnotes
Reference citations and supplementary information at the bottom of a page.
formatting
The process of designing a book for electronic distribution, with the desired layout, fonts, and appearance. *Compare:* typesetting.
forum
An online place where people with common interests or backgrounds come together to find and share information and discuss topics of interest.
front list
Traditional term for books in their first year of publication.
front matter
The sections of a book preceding the first chapter. *Also:* prelims. *Compare:* back matter.
full-service distribution
Wholesalers and distributors who perform a broad range of services,

such as stocking inventories, operating warehouses, supplying credit, and employing salespeople, as well as delivering goods.

G

galley copy
See: proof.

genre
A general category for a creative work, such as romance, science fiction, mystery.

ghostwriting
Writing all or part of a book on behalf of a collaborator whose name will be listed as the author.

go direct
To publish books to a retailer without the use of an intermediary service like an aggregator or distributor.

Goodreads
A social media site owned by Amazon, which is just for books. Readers connect with friends, get book recommendations, write reviews, and make reading lists.

Goodreads advertising
Pay-per-click advertising on Goodreads.

Goodreads giveaway
An online book giveaway that any Goodreads member can enter.

Google Adwords
Text-based ads that show up next to Google search results, graphic display ads that show up on websites or apps, or YouTube video ads that show up during videos.

Google Play
An ebook retailer which, although still in operation, has been closed to new authors for several years and is not expected to reopen.

Google Preview
Google Play's interface for viewing excerpts of an ebook before purchase. *Compare:* Look Inside the Book.

go wide
To sell books through a variety of retailers; the opposite of exclusivity, in which books are sold through one retailer.
greyscale
A color model that uses only shades of black. *See also:* CMYK, RGB.
guest blogging
Writing a post or short article for someone else's blog.

H

halftone
A method of representing an image with dots of varying sizes.
hardback/hardcover
A book with a hard rather than paper cover; or the cover itself.
hard return
Pressing the enter or return key to force a line break instead of allowing the text to flow naturally.
hashtag
A word or phrase immediately preceded by the # symbol. When you click a hashtag, you see other social media updates containing the same keyword or topic.
headshot
A professional-looking head-and-shoulders photograph used for promotional purposes.
hit
Accessing a web page or a file, image, or script on the page.
house ad
A self-promotional ad that you run on your own website to sell your own products.
hybrid author
An author who uses both trade and self-publishing services. (Not to be confused with hybrid publishing or partnership publishing.)
hybrid publishing
See: partnership publishing.

hyphen
Connects two things that are intimately related, usually words that work together as a single concept or joint modifier (e.g. self-publishing, two-thirds).

I

iBooks
The iBooks Store, an online publisher/retailer for ebooks. Also the application used to read books downloaded from the iBooks Store.

impression
A single display of an advertisement or web page.

imprint
A name used by a publisher to identify their books. Imprints are frequently genre-specific, and a single publisher may have multiple imprints.

inbound marketing
A model that relies on the initiative of customers to find and purchase a product, such as content marketing, social media marketing, and search engine optimization.

independent
Not involving the "Big Five" publishing corporations; self-published.

InDesign
Professional book formatting and design software produced by Adobe.

index
A list directing readers to specific subject matter in a book.

indie author
An author who acts as the creative director of their own books, whether through self-publishing, assisted self-publishing, or traditional publishing. *Compare:* self-publishing, traditional publishing.

Indie Author Fringe
Free online author conference organized three times a year by the

Alliance of Independent Authors, fringe to London Book Fair, Book Expo America, and Frankfurt Book Fair.

Ingram ipage
An online books search, order, and account management platform for bookstores.

IngramSpark
A large publisher and distributor of print-on-demand books and ebooks.

initial coin offering (ICO)
An unregulated means of crowdfunding by which money is raised for a new cryptocurrency, selling tokens in the currency to raise money.

Instafreebie
A streamlined way to send book copies to reviewers, beta readers, or bloggers by providing a link for people to download your book for free.

interior
All content within a book, except the covers. *Compare:* book block.

IPR License
Platform for authors, publishers, and agents to list and license publishing rights, providing access to a global marketplace. Owned by Frankfurt Book Fair with the Copyright Clearance Center.

ISBN (International Standard Book Number)
A unique, numeric identifier for a particular edition and format of a book.

J

jacket
See dust jacket.

joint venture
See: partnership publishing.

JPEG
A format for compressing image files; the most common image format used by digital cameras.

K

KDP Select
An optional program under Kindle Direct Publishing that requires exclusivity in exchange for promotional tools and enrollment in Kindle Unlimited and Kindle Owners' Lending Library.

keyword
A word or phrase used by search engines to identify matching subjects. For example, an edition of *Moby Dick* might have the keywords *whaling, revenge,* and *nautical themes.*

Kindle
Amazon's line of proprietary ebook readers.

Kindleboards
An online discussion forum dedicated to publishing on Amazon.

Kindle Direct Publishing (KDP)
Amazon's publishing and distribution platform for ebooks.

Kindle Owners' Lending Library (KOLL)
A program under Kindle Direct Publishing that allows Amazon Prime subscribers to read one free ebook per month. Enrollment in KOLL is mandatory for KDP Select authors. *See also:* Kindle Unlimited (KU).

Kindle Scout
An Amazon program in which readers nominate books for publication under the Kindle Press imprint. Winners receive a five-year contract, 50% royalties, and a $1,500 advance.

Kindle Singles
Amazon's digital, curated imprint for short works (primarily novellas, short fiction, and long-form journalism).

Kindle Unlimited (KU)
A program under Kindle Direct Publishing that allows subscribers to read ebooks in the KU catalog for free. Enrollment in KU is mandatory for KDP Select authors. *See also:* Kindle Owners' Lending Library.

Kindle Worlds
Amazon's digital publishing platform for fan fiction.

Kobo
A Toronto-based digital publishing platform, initially meant to
service users of the Kobo e-reader.

L

launch party
Celebration of the publication of a book. Can be hosted at any
suitable location, but popular spots include bookstores, libraries,
coffee shops, or the author's home. You can also host a virtual book
launch online.

LCCN (Library of Congress Control Number)
A unique identifier assigned to books by the US Library of Congress.
Compare: ISBN.

legacy publishing
A somewhat derogatory term for trade-publishing.

license
Legal permission granted to someone other than the original holder
of a right; for example, permitting a publisher to print a work for
which you hold the copyright. *Compare:* copyright.

limited edition
A book printed in limited numbers, usually for special editions.

line editing
See: copyediting.

list price
The recommended retail price of a book. Set by the author or
publisher and often referred to as the RRP.

literary agent
Person who acts as an intermediary for an author in transactions with
the publisher.

litho printing (lithography)
A method of mass-production printing using wet ink and printing
plates. More suitable for longer runs. *See also:* offset printing.
Compare: digital printing.

Look Inside the Book

An Amazon feature that allows customers to view excerpts from an ebook or print book before buying. *Compare:* Google Preview.

M

makeready stage

Point in the printing process when a text is ready to be printed.

manuscript

Complete version of a book (often as an electronic text file) prepared by the author.

manuscript appraisal

See: content editing.

manuscript conversion

See: conversion.

marketing plan

A strategic plan that details all of the activities you need to deliver to promote yourself and your book.

mass-market paperback

Smaller, less expensive version of a book that is usually printed well after the hardcover and trade paperback versions have been made available.

media kit

A package of key information to send to media or journalists, retailers, book bloggers, event planners, editors, or anyone who plans on writing about you and your book. May include an author photo and bio, a book cover image, a full synopsis, a one-sentence description, book details, frequently asked questions, an excerpt, and reviews or media coverage.

media list

A collection of media outlets and contacts that you reach out to in order to increase awareness of your book.

media outlet

Any channel for disseminating news about your book, such as newspapers, magazines, radio shows, TV shows, online news sites, podcasts, or blogs.

metadata
The details of a book other than its actual text, such as author's name, publisher, book description, ISBN, and keywords.

micropayments
Financial transactions of very small sums of money.

MOBI
Amazon's digital format for Kindle ebooks.

N

NetGalley
An online book reviewing site. Book reviewers, librarians, booksellers, educators, and media professionals request complimentary ebooks in exchange for reviews.

networking
Using and expanding your social network or sphere of influence to promote your book.

newswire distribution
Circulation of news through a service intended for journalists and media outlets.

niche
A specialized target market characterized by a particular interest, topic, or subject.

Nielsen
The sole registrar for ISBNs in the UK and Ireland.

nonexclusive contract
Legal agreement in which the publisher does not exercise exclusive rights over the materials published in your book.

Nook
Barnes & Noble's line of e-readers and associated retailer.

O

offset printing
A method of mass-production printing in which the images on metal plates are transferred (offset) onto rubber blankets or rollers and thereby to paper. *Compare:* digital printing.

off-the-book-page attention
Mention made of a book outside the context of a book review, such as plugging a book on a talk show.

online bookseller/retailer
Internet-based bookstore.

online marketing
Using online methods to advertise, sell, or dispense products.

OUTIA (Open Up To Indie Authors)
Alliance of Independent Authors campaign encouraging bookstores, libraries, reviewing bodies, literary events, and prizes to find ways to include self-publishing writers in their programs. Uses the hashtag #PublishingOpenUp.

out of print (OOP)
Book no longer in a publisher's book inventory (and for which there is no reprint planned).

P

P2P lending
P2P means peer-to-peer, or person-to-person, and refers to anything decentralized and direct. P2P lending is loaning money to individuals without the systems and processes typically used by traditional financial institutions. Instead, it is often handled by digital platforms that use an algorithm to manage transactions between parties.

paperback
A book bound in stiff paper or flexible card. *See also:* mass-market paperback, trade paperback.

partnership publishing
A publishing arrangement in which the author and the publisher both contribute financially to the book's production, sharing risks and rewards. Sometimes used as a euphemism for vanity publishing. *See also:* joint venture, hybrid publishing, self-publishing services, shared publishing, subsidized publishing.

pay per click
See: cost per click

pay per impression
See: cost per impression

pbook
A physical, printed book generally constructed of a number of sheets of paper, bound in cardboard. *See also:* codex.

PDF (portable document format)
A file format popular for its cross-compatibility, particularly in keeping layout and fonts as intended. The preferred file format for print-on-demand and fixed layout ebooks.

perfect bound
An unsewn binding where glue/adhesive attaches the pages at the spine. Usually with a paper cover, hence the more common name paperback. *Compare:* hardback.

permafree
A book permanently available for free from online retailers; a strategy used to increase visibility and gain new readers by giving away a book, often the first in a series.

permission
Agreement from a copyright holder that permits the reproduction or publication of copyrighted material. Also the process of securing agreements from copyright holder.

permissioned blockchain
Blockchain with access restricted to a particular group. *Compare:* unpermissioned blockchain.

pitch emails
Emails targeting media contacts to get coverage for a book, which should include key points about the book and author.

plant costs
Initial costs incurred by a traditional printer in preparation for the first printing run of a given title.

platform
The computer hardware or online system used to run a program or digital tool.

plot
Flow or succession of actions in a story.

podcast
Online audio broadcast available on a website or to download.

prelims
Pages before a book properly begins. May include copyright page, table of contents, acknowledgments, and other publishing information. *Also:* front matter. *Compare:* back matter.

pre-order
A marketing tactic used by authors to offer readers the opportunity of reserving a copy of a book prior to its official release date.

press release
An official announcement that provides information about an event to reporters, bloggers, and other media outlets.

Prime Reading
A program that allows Amazon Prime subscribers to read free ebooks from a catalog of approximately 1,000 titles selected by Amazon.

print-on-demand (POD)
Printing in small quantities or as needed, usually by digital printing.

print ready
Used to describe the final layout file of a book, usually in PDF format, that is ready to go to the printer.

print run
The number of copies printed in a single order.

Pronoun
A now defunct ebook publisher and aggregator.

proof
A copy of a book printed for final inspection and correction of errors. *Also:* galley copy. *Compare:* advance review copy.

proofreading
The final step in the editing process, with a focus on essential corrections such as misspellings, the accuracy of captions, headings, page numbers, etc.

publication date
Official date when a book is to be released to the public.

publicist
Professional or press agent who promotes a book, often by generating free advertising.

publicity tour
Public circuit an author makes to publicize a book, either prior to or soon after the publication date.

PubMatch
Rights management platform that allows authors and publishers to trade publishing rights and permissions with publishers, agents, and other rights buyers. Owned by the London Book Fair.

Q

QR code
A machine-readable code that consists of black and white squares and is typically used for storing URLs.

R

region
A geographical area served by a retailer. For example, Amazon operates separate regional websites for the US, Canada, Mexico, the UK, India, France, Germany, China, Japan, Italy, Spain, the Netherlands, Australia, and Brazil. *Also:* territory.

remainder
A book returned to the publisher after not having sold, often offered for later sale at a discounted price.

return
A book returned to the publisher and refunded after failing to sell in a bookstore.

reversion
The process of reclaiming rights licensed to a publisher.

review
A customer's opinion of a book published on a retailer website or similar venue. *Compare:* editorial review.

RGB
A color model for digital and online use, using red, green, and blue. *See also:* CMYK, greyscale.

rights/publishing rights
The right to publish or produce a book, TV show, film, translation, or other format based on your material, in a particular medium or a particular territory. Granted to the publisher/producer by license.

ROI (return on investment)
The amount you spend versus how much money you earn.

royalties
A percentage of book sales paid to the author. Often used interchangeably with commission.

S

saddlestitch binding
Pages are bound along the fold with two staples.

sales funnel
A process that converts your website and social media visitors into paying readers by convincing them to purchase your books.

sales handle
A one-sentence call to action epitomizing your book, which is frequently used in online marketing.

sales rank
A ranking calculated by Amazon on the basis of daily sales and downloads of a book. *Also:* bestseller rank.

Scrivener
Popular editing and organizational software designed specifically for writers.

secondary rights
The right to resell a work after its first publication.

self-publishing
A form of publishing in which the author oversees the publishing process, retains control over creative decisions and disposition of publishing rights, and bears the costs of production.

self-publishing service
A company or freelancer commissioned by an author to provide any of the seven processes involved in publishing a book: editorial, design, production, distribution, marketing, promotion, or rights service. Some companies offer a full-service package. *Compare*: partnership publishing.

sell sheet
See: advance information sheet.

SEO (search engine optimization)
The process of making your web page more easily findable and indexed by search engines; or more relevant to particular topics in order to attract more visitors.

shared publishing
See: partnership publishing.

shelf life
The time an unsold book remains on the shelf of a retail store before being replaced by fresh or better-selling stock.

short discount
Smaller-than-typical discount on books purchased by retailers and wholesalers.

short-run print
Printing of a limited number of copies of a book in a single print run. Can now be as low as 300–400 copies. For fewer copies, digital printing is generally a better option.

slush pile
The unsolicited manuscripts submitted to a traditional publisher.

small press
Smaller publishing house that releases books often intended for specialized audiences.

smart contracts
Computer programs that automatically execute legally binding contracts. These automated and often blockchain-based computer protocols facilitate, verify, or enforce digital agreements, saving time and reducing costs in common legal and financial transactions and potentially replacing lawyers and banks.

Smashwords
A popular ebook publisher and aggregator.

special sales
Book sales through nonbookstore outlets such as restaurants, gift stores, and health spas.

spine width
Width of part of the book that is visible on a bookshelf. The spine connects the front and back covers.

spiral bound
A method of binding in which wire or plastic is wound through holes punched along the side of a book.

split A/B test
Comparing two versions of something to see which performs better (sometimes called split testing).

structural edit
See: developmental editing.

style sheet
Document prepared during copyediting that records consistency and style decisions, such as how numbers, abbreviations, word usage, and punctuation are to be handled.

subscript
A character (number, letter, or symbol) that is set slightly below the normal line of type. It is usually smaller than the rest of the text.

subsidiary right
The right to publish a work based on the original material but in a

different format (e.g. translations, audiobooks, film). *Also:* subright or sublease.

subsidized publishing
See: partnership publishing.

superscript
A character (number, letter, or symbol) that is set slightly above the normal line of type. It is usually smaller than the rest of the text.

synopsis
A summary introducing your main characters, the main conflict, and the basic emotional arc of your story.

T

table of contents
A list, usually in the front matter, of the book's chapters or main sections and their opening page numbers.

target audience
A specific audience that is most likely to buy your books and is usually based on demographic information or areas of interest.

termination clause
Section in a contractual agreement that specifies particular behavior, actions, or events that would result in nullification of the contract.

territory
See: region.

thumbnail
A small representation of a larger image, intended as a preview.

token
A type of security issued in digital form. For example, a READ token gives the owner the right to read an ebook.

trade paperback
A book bound with a paper or heavy stock cover, usually with a larger trim size than that of a mass-market paperback.

trade-publisher (traditional publisher)
A company that invests in publishing a manuscript, submitted by an

author, and controls most creative and marketing decisions. Trade-publishers bear the cost of production and promotion in exchange for a sizable percentage (typically 90%+) of the receipts from a book.

trim size
The dimensions of a print book, specifically the page size.

Tweep
Followers on the social media platform Twitter.

Twitter handle
The name, always preceded by @, that is used on the social media platform Twitter.

typeface
A set of letters, numbers, and characters that are all in the same style and that are used in printing. *Compare:* font.

typesetting
Professional preparation of a book for print with the desired layout, fonts, and appearance. *Compare:* formatting.

U

unit cost
The production or base cost of printing and putting together a book.

unique visitor (unique)
An individual who accesses a website. *Compare:* hit.

universal link
A link that allows you to simplify the process of author discoverability by directing your book customers to your preferred online retailer.

university press
Publishing house owned and operated by a university. Such presses typically issue academic material, often including works by their own academics.

unpermissioned blockchain
Blockchain open to all.

unsolicited manuscript
Manuscript sent to a publisher who did not request it.

URL (uniform resource locator)
The address of a web page.

V

vanity publishing (press)
A generally exploitative form of publishing in which the author pays to have their book published, with excessively high fees and substandard service. *Compare:* partnership publishing.

virtual book tour (VBT)
Advertisement strategy centered on publicizing a book on the internet, including ads on websites that the target audience frequents and book giveaways.

vlogging
A blog that contains video content. This growing segment of the blogosphere is sometimes referred to as the vlogosphere.

W

wholesaler
A company that sells books to retailers, often in bulk and at a discount.

word of mouth
Publicity through recommendations from friends, family, and associates.

ABOUT THE AUTHOR

Debbie Young

Like Alice down the rabbit-hole, I fell into self-publishing more or less by accident. In a career spent in journalism, public relations, and marketing, my brief was always to build understanding between my employers and their target audiences. A significant birthday provided the wake-up call to get round to what I'd always wanted to do when I grew up: write books.

Having joined ALLi almost as soon as it was formed, I welcomed Orna's invitation in 2013 to become commissioning editor of its Self-Publishing Author Advice Center blog. I'm now an ambassador and evangelist for the movement, speaking at public events and writing for other publications to raise awareness.

Meanwhile I've been practicing what I preach, self-publishing a professionally produced body of fiction, including a new series of classic mystery novels plus a mixed range of nonfiction, and founding the Hawkesbury Upton Literature Festival to showcase authors of all kinds.

As co-author of *Opening Up to Indie Authors*, I've found enormous satisfaction in deploying the skills and experience gained in my previous career for the good of the self-publishing movement. I hope and believe that this book will foster better understanding and cooperation between indie authors and all sectors of the publishing trade, and decimate misplaced resentment, helping to shape a brighter future for us all.

Orna Ross (Series Editor)

I was born and raised in Ireland and now live in London and St Leonards-on-Sea, England. I worked for twenty years in media and publishing, and published fiction and nonfiction with both small and trade-publishing houses before taking my rights back and striking out as an indie author in 2011. The radically empowering experience of publishing my own work led me to form the Alliance of Independent Authors in 2012, work for which UK publishing trade magazine, the *Bookseller*, has kindly listed me as one of their Top 100 people in publishing. This is a tribute to the dedication of the wonderful ALLi team and all our members (ALLis, pronounced "allies").

OTHER BOOKS FROM ALLI

ALLi Successful Self-Publishing Series

1: Creative Self-Publishing: How Indie Authors Publish for Pleasure and Profit by Orna Ross

2: Choosing the Best Self-Publishing Companies and Services by Jim Giammatteo and John Doppler

3: How Authors Sell Publishing Rights by Helen Sedwick and Orna Ross

ALLi Campaign Series

Opening Up to Indie Authors by Debbie Young and Dan Holloway

Blockchain for Books by Orna Ross and Sukhi Jutla

OUR ADVICE TO YOUR INBOX?

Sign up here for a weekly round-up from our self-publishing advice blog:
    selfpublishingadvice.org/signup

REVIEW REQUEST

If you enjoyed this book, please consider leaving a brief review online at the retailers' site where you purchased it, on social media, and on your website, to help make it more discoverable for other authors.

Printed in Great Britain
by Amazon

49100677R00099